ADHD 2.0
&
SOCIAL ANXIETY
FOR ADULTS

THE 7-DAY REVOLUTION
OVERCOME ATTENTION DEFICIT DISORDER
SOCIAL SKILLS | SELF-DISCIPLINE | FOCUS MASTERY | HABITS
WIN FRIENDS & ACHIEVE GOALS TO SUCCESS

MARGARET HAMPTON

CONTENTS

ABOUT THE AUTHOR

Margaret Hampton is an author, cognitive behavioral counselor, and speaker with more than 20 years of clinical practice. Her books have impacted the lives of adults with ADHD every day. They offer a comprehensive look into ADHD, including everything from real-life stories to management tools and advice for dealing with a close person who has ADHD.

Besides being professionally involved in the topic, Ms. Hampton is also an ADHD individual herself and her children. She has extensive work and knowledge in recognizing and coping with ADHD.

At her conferences, Ms. Hampton always offers timeless, research-backed advice and solutions applicable to adults and children. She highlights the most significant challenges and combines traditional treatment with contemporary treatment.

Mrs. Hampton, within her books, proves that ADHD can be an invaluable asset in one person's life and she proves it throughout many examples. She has become an amazing painter herself, as a consequence of her neurodiversity's imagination and creativity, turning a disorder into a little life achievement.

INTRODUCTION

If you put me at a big celebration, business, or charity event, I will instinctively walk toward the people in the room who have ADHD. This is not on purpose. It simply occurs that way. It isn't because I have the expertise and wrote this book or because I've worked in this sector for more than 20 years. It's not because two of my three kids have ADHD. It's because I intuitively recognize my community. I, too, suffer from ADHD, but you probably wouldn't see it initially.

Unless you know where to look, the signs of ADHD are generally invisible. Most people wouldn't realize that I have trouble sitting because I don't fidget much and don't get up and walk about when I do not need to. Instead, I keep myself entertained by wearing jewelry that I can fiddle with or follow the ridges of the glass with my palm. In social circumstances, you might not see all of the ways I'm trying to fit in or that it takes a lot of work to appear "normal."

I am always working hard to hide my ADHD inclinations by seeming to care about polite small conversation, not interrupting others, and intently listening. I have been thinking about my behavior for years. It is wrong! I had to make something, a change that would help me overcome my issues and be better, not make me hide my inclinations. So yes, this book is also about social anxiety or the anxiety that comes from ADHD.

The combination of appearing to be an adult and hog-tying random thoughts and acts eventually leads to social tiredness. So I gravitate toward those who are mischievous and interruptive like myself. Discussions with other people who have ADHD swing around various themes in a freestyle flow of consciousness. I'm no longer trying to blend in. I'm not very concerned with ADHD symptoms. I'm in the moment, loving the party, getting to know my ADHD self, and relieving the anxiety I feel.

You might not realize how ADHD impacts me daily unless you spend time with me. You may notice that I struggle to recall things, pay attention in meetings, listen to instructions, and complete activities. You're highly likely to observe me searching for missing objects while muttering, "Now, where might that be?" If you don't know that there are indications of ADHD, you could dismiss me as careless, disorganized, untrustworthy, or even stupid. People frequently misinterpret ADHD symptoms as character qualities rather than neurological anomalies.

I know a lot of people do not understand ADHD. I also know that they misunderstand the signs they perceive. I try to appear "normal," which necessitates me faking it. Every day, I struggle with seemingly straightforward activities in life. For example, I'd want to call and meet a friend for coffee, but anything that isn't already occurring seems too big to organize. Some days, I feel I can't gather my scattered ideas long enough to begin a task, remain on track, and complete it.

My attempts to suppress my symptoms frequently fail horribly. Little ADHD mistakes accumulate during the day: I double-book customers, struggle to pay a bill, or leave my vehicle windows open on a wet day. I'm fatigued and feel like a failure by the evening, and I'm sure others perceive me as a failure.

I'm all too aware of how those of us with ADHD are seen by the non-ADHD world. Previous bosses, acquaintances, and even family members have misinterpreted my symptoms as carelessness, sloth, or incompetence. Even when others are aware that I have ADHD, they frequently link my symptoms to character defects, asking me to pay more attention to this or that.

I routinely talk to various organisations about the effects of ADHD on individuals. I spoke to a large group of parents about parenting emotionally stable ADHD children on one such occasion. I stressed the significance of teaching their children problem-solving skills during the lesson. I described how quickly people with ADHD experience feelings of guilt and inadequacy. Following that, some of the parents formed a queue to ask further questions, and I assisted the participants in developing their next steps in parenting. At the stage, a well-meaning non-ADHD parent approached me and said, "I'll have your glass. I'm sure you'll forget to do it," then grinned and laughed. I must have appeared surprised since she came to a halt and asked, "Did you need this glass?" Her comments had hit me square in the face. She'd thought I'd forget and made a joke out of my difficulties, delivering the all-too-familiar jab, "I'll do this for you since you're too careless to do it." I had previously planned for my carelessness by placing the remote control I was using next to the glass so I wouldn't lose it.

I thought about how quickly I might feel incompetent on the way home. I hoped the woman had just stated, "I would be delighted to take care of this for you." I know she didn't try to deliver the negative impression that I was irresponsible, but people with ADHD are bombarded with these subtle signals. They accumulate and create dents in our feeling of well-being.

Part of the difficulty stems from how people see me, but another aspect is how harshly I criticise myself. I am sensitive to criticism and judgment, as are many people with ADHD. I make the cognitive error of seeing criticism where it is not intended, like with the helpful parent at the meeting.

I've attempted to conceal my natural way of thinking or behaving from others to fit into a non-ADHD environment. To assist me in blending in, I researched the characteristics of non-ADHD people's thinking and behavior. I've decided that I can no longer pretend to be neurotypical.

Instead, I need to be open about how ADHD impacts me, how I think, and how I behave, and then utilize that knowledge to assist me in navigating the environment in which I live. It's a never-ending game of adapting, but it works! I don't have to act any longer. I recognize that I am unique compared to people who do not have ADHD. And – despite living in a fast-paced, complex world full of interruptions – I can navigate by constantly gaining new skills and attitudes. Learning how my brain works allow me to devise hacks and workarounds to get things done and be kind to myself when I don't.

If you have ADHD, you must understand that your brain is not damaged. Your brain is wired differently and does not function similarly to a "normal" or neurotypical brain. Compared to the non-ADHD brain, some portions of the ADHD brain are hyperactive, while others are underactive. Understanding, accepting, and compensating for our differences is much easier when we see how the ADHD brain differs from the neurotypical brain.

The realisation that ADHD is a complex condition that impacts all aspects of a person's life is the first step in managing it. I hope you will learn to recognize your ADHD habits and make the required adjustments to live productively. The information you will receive will help you live more efficiently. The knowledge you will receive about ADHD will allow you to manage your symptoms without having to fake them to others or yourself.

WHY SHOULD I EXPECT THIS BOOK TO BE HELPFUL TO ME?

This question is valid; however, as with many topics with ADHD, the answer is complex.

To begin, the majority of the coping strategies I will address in this book are likely to be similar, if not the same, to those found in the numerous popular publications that advise on managing adult ADHD. ADHD is not a lack of information problem; instead, it is a productivity problem—being unable to execute what you set out to do consistently.

Second, since ADHD is a problem with skill performance, the resemblance of coping methods and practices across various books and programs and the repeated information is not bad. To be more specific, having numerous and varied remembrances of these techniques helps to refresh the significance of these routines in your life constantly.

The combination of skill review and somewhat diverse presentations of these concepts across multiple mediums adds a level of freshness and offers new perspectives on old themes. The diversified presentation of ideas and teachings, just as in learning, enhances the possibility that these notions will "stick" and come back up during everyday life when you need them the most. Diet and fitness books routinely rank among the top sales each year – not because earlier books did not give valuable advice – because changing these behaviors is tough.

In terms of your willingness to adapt, my method expects a lot from you. Coping methods and take-away notes are important tools, but they are not unchanging laws of physics. You must employ them so they can be effective. You must be willing to confront and suspend your concerns about your power to transform and reduce your social anxiety.

CHAPTER 1
UNDERSTANDING ADHD

This chapter focuses on ADHD and all the general information you need to know. This information will assist you in determining whether or not the step-by-step methods and techniques featured in this book are appropriate for you. You will learn how to comprehend the features of adult ADHD, discover why ADHD symptoms persist in adults and understand that ADHD is a genuine adult diagnosis.

Attention deficit/hyperactivity disorder (ADHD) is a recognized medical and mental condition. ADHD manifests itself in childhood, and many children with ADHD have significant symptoms as adults. People experience three basic types of signs: poor focus, hyperactivity, and impulsivity.

Many individuals with ADHD have at least some hyperactivity, poor attention, and impulsivity, while many people have symptoms predominantly from one group. Attention Deficit Disorder (ADD) is used when an individual has selective attention symptoms but not hyperactive symptoms.

People with ADHD can develop coping techniques to help them deal with the problems that come with the disorder. ADHD is a neurological illness that has nothing to do with intelligence, aptitude, laziness, being insane or not, and so on. The treatment plan – which usually begins after an individual takes ADHD drugs for many months – can help adults regulate their ADHD symptoms. You will see big changes if you actively study skills and practice them regularly.

A mental health practitioner will usually diagnose ADHD based on the definition of the American Psychiatric Association's Diagnostic and Statistical Manual of Mental Disorders (DSM). The DSM, besides anxiety disorders, features bipolar disorders, feeding and eating disorders, depressive disorders, and compulsive personality disorders. The DSM-5 includes all of the different mental illnesses and the symptoms and other criteria that an individual must exhibit to be diagnosed with them.

Individuals must demonstrate at least five of the nine potential inattention symptoms and/or five of the nine potential impulsivity/ hyperactivity symptoms to fulfill the DSM- 5 criteria for adult ADHD. Individuals with ADHD – mostly inattentive presentation – show five or more symptoms in the inattention group.

ADHD – mainly impulsive/ hyperactive presentation – is defined as five or more symptoms in the impulsivity/hyperactivity group (Hallowell, 2022). Those who have five or more symptoms from both groups have ADHD with a mixed presentation. The inability to pay attention to details, trouble sustaining attention in tasks, appearing not to listen when spoken to immediately, failing to adhere to commands, problems with organization, denial of activities that require prolonged mental effort, regularly losing things, easily confused, and forgetfulness are all examples of inattentive symptoms. Fidgeting, departing one's seat repeatedly, feelings of restlessness, inability to participate in peaceful tasks, being "on the move," chatting incessantly, blurting out replies, having difficulties waiting in lines, and constantly interrupting are all hyperactive/impulsive symptoms.

Furthermore, the person must have had at least some of the symptoms before 12, and the symptoms must be present in approximately two different situations. The symptoms must interact with the person's ability to act, and another mental disorder must not better explain the symptoms.

HOW DO WE TELL THE DIFFERENCE BETWEEN ADHD AND NORMAL FUNCTIONING?

Some of the symptoms described above sound normal. Most individuals would undoubtedly admit to being easily distracted or having difficulty organising themselves. This is true for a large number of mental illnesses. For example, everyone experiences sadness from time to time, but not everyone fits the criteria for clinical depression.

To be diagnosed with ADHD, an individual must be experiencing severe difficulty in some element of their life, such as job, school, or interaction patterns. In DSM-5, there is a greater emphasis on impairment particular to adults, such as impairment at work.

In addition, ADHD must drive the person's suffering and disability and not by another illness to qualify for the diagnosis. A comprehensive evaluation is required to eliminate the possibility that the symptoms result from another psychological disease.

HOW DO COGNITIVE AND BEHAVIORAL FACTORS CONTRIBUTE TO ADULT ADHD?

Cognitive components (thoughts and beliefs) might exacerbate ADHD symptoms. For instance, if a person is confronted with something he would find overwhelming, he may divert his focus elsewhere or say things like, "I can't do this," "I don't want this," or "I will do this later." The behavioral components are what people do that might aggravate ADHD symptoms. Actual behaviors might include delaying doing what you should be doing or maintaining or discontinuing an organizing structure.

It is no secret that the primary symptoms of ADHD are biological. Nevertheless, researchers think cognitive and behavioral factors also influence symptom levels (Hallowell, 2022).

Core neuropsychiatric deficits limit successful coping beginning in childhood. Adults with ADHD have been suffering from the illness since infancy. Distractibility, disorganization, trouble following through on activities, and impulsivity are all characteristics that can impede individuals with ADHD from learning or practicing appropriate coping techniques.

Individuals with this disease generally have chronic underachievement or other experiences that they may characterize as "failures." Due to this history of failure, individuals with ADHD may acquire unduly negative ideas about themselves and negative, dysfunctional thinking while approaching activities. The negative thoughts and attitudes might contribute to avoidance or attention deficits. When presented with tasks or issues that they find difficult or dull, individuals with ADHD divert their attention even more, and accompanying behavioral symptoms might worsen.

DOES MEDICATION TREAT ADHD SUCCESSFULLY?

Yes. Medications are presently the first-line therapy option for adult ADHD, and they have received the greatest research attention. These drugs fall into four categories: stimulants, monoamine oxidase inhibitors, tricyclic antidepressants, and atypical antidepressants.

However, a significant proportion of people who take antidepressants (about 20% to 50%) are nonresponders. A nonresponder is someone whose symptoms are not adequately lessened or who cannot tolerate the drugs. Furthermore, those considered responders often demonstrate a decrease in just 50% or fewer of the primary symptoms of ADHD (Hallowell, 2022).

Thanks to these findings, guidelines for the optimal treatment of adult ADHD include combining psychotherapy (particularly cognitive-behavioral therapy) with medicines. Many of the main symptoms of ADHD, such as focus issues, hyperactivity, and impulsivity, can be reduced with medication.

ADULT ADHD IS A REAL MEDICAL CONDITION

ADHD in adulthood is a real, reliable medical disorder that affects up to 5% of people in the United States. Adult ADHD has always been a contentious diagnosis. One explanation for this is that psychiatric diagnoses are difficult to validate. Specialists can do blood work, x-rays, biopsies, or even take a patient's temperature to aid in making a diagnosis in many different medical professions. In some circumstances, overt medical proof supplements the patient's narrative.

However, for psychological problems, these tests are currently impossible. Doctors must diagnose psychiatric diseases solely on their patients' self-reported symptoms, their observations of the patient, or the views of others. Psychiatrists and psychologists have devised a method for classifying mental diseases by examining groupings of exhibited symptoms.

Sufficient scientific data has been collected over the last few decades, concluding that ADHD is a genuine, substantial, stressful, interfering, and valid medical disease. This data includes proof that ADHD can be diagnosed reliably in adults (Hallowell, 2022) and that the diagnosis fulfills diagnostic validity requirements comparable to those of other psychiatric illnesses. Key symptoms in adulthood include difficulties with attention, inhibition, and self-regulation. These basic symptoms result in adult limitations such as the following:

• Poor school and work performance (difficulty with the organization or making plans, becoming distracted, insufficient sustained attention to reading and documentation, procrastination, poor time management, and rash decision making).

• Impaired interpersonal skills (e.g., friendship problems, poor follow-through on responsibilities, poor listening skills, various difficulties with intimate relationships).

• Problems with behavior (for example, those with ADHD end up less educated, have issues with money management, have difficulty managing their house, and have chaotic routines).

• Medication treatment research and genetic investigations that include adoption and family studies, neurochemistry research, and neuroimaging provide additional support for the validity of ADHD as a diagnosis.

ADHD affects between 1% and 5% of individuals. This percentage is comparable with estimations that ADHD affects (Weiss & Hechtman, 1993) 2% to 9% of school-age children, and follow-up studies of ADHD children suggest that debilitating ADHD symptoms remain into adulthood (beyond puberty) in 30% to 80% of diagnosed children.

THE ADHD PEOPLE

A problem child that makes its parents insane by being completely disorganized, incapable of following through on almost anything, not capable of cleaning up a room, doing household chores, or performing just about any given task; the one who is constantly interrupting, looking for excuses for a job not done, and usually operating far below potential. We're the child who gets lectured regularly about how we're squandering our skills, squandering the great chance that our intrinsic aptitude offers us to succeed, and failing to use what our parents have given us properly.

We are also the talented executives who consistently fall short due to missed deadlines, forgotten duties, social faux pas, and squandered chances. We are too frequently the addicts, misfits, jobless, and criminals who are just one diagnosis and treatment plan away from turning our lives around. We are the individuals for whom Marlon Brando declared in the famous 1954 film On the Waterfront, "I could become a contender." So many could have and should have, been contenders.

But we can also make amends. We are the seemingly uninterested meeting attendee who appears out of nowhere with a novel idea that saves the day. We are frequently the "underachieving" adults whose ability blossoms with the proper type of assistance and achieves impressive success despite a shaky school record. We are the competitors as well as the winners.

We're also creative and dynamic instructors, preachers, circus perform-ers, stand-up comedians, Navy SEALs or Army Rangers, innovators, tinkerers, and trend setters. There are self-made multimillionaires among us, Pulitzer and Nobel prize winners, Academy, Grammy, Tony, Emmy award winners, top-tier trial attorneys, neurosurgeons, commodities market traders, and stockbrokers (Weiss & Hechtman, 1993). And we are frequently business owners. We are businessmen, and most adult ADHD patients we meet are or desire to be business owners. Dan Sullivan – the founder and owner of a business assistance organization called Strategic Coach – has ADHD and believes that at least half of his customers have ADHD.

Because individuals with ADHD don't stand out from the crowd, our disease is almost unnoticed. However, if you were to crawl into our thoughts, you would find a different scene. Ideas would fly around like kernels in a popcorn machine, rat-a-tat rapidly and on no discernible schedule. Ideas come in random, unpredictable spurts. Since we can't turn off this specific popcorn machine, we're frequently unable to halt the formation of ideas at night. Our thoughts never seem to rest.

Indeed, our brains are here, there, and just about everywhere simultane-ously, which occasionally emerges as the appearance of being someplace else, in some dreaming condition. It is not a secret that we frequently miss the metaphorical boat, but maybe we should construct an aircraft or get a pogo stick instead. We tune out during a job interview and don't get the job, but perhaps we spot a poster in the human resource depart-ment waiting area that inspires a fresh idea that leads to a patented innovation.

We upset others by forgetting names and commitments, but we make amends by recognizing something no one else has noticed. We shoot ourselves in the foot only to invent a painless means of removing the bullet on the spot. "It can be the individuals' no one can envision anything of who perform the things no one can imagine," stated the famous mathematician Alan Turing. That describes us.

ADHD is a more prosperous, more intricate, precarious, and possibly beneficial state of being than neurotypical people would believe and what diagnostic tests (Weiss & Hechtman, 1993) would have you believe.

The word "ADHD" refers to a manner of being in the world. It is a collection of characteristics unique to a particular type of mind and may be a significant benefit based on how a person controls it.

After covering ADHD, and its essential features, we need to focus on something else. As someone with ADHD, you probably already know "anxiety." I also think that you know the word social and how it is related to anxiety. Let's learn what social anxiety is and what the two of them can do to someone.

CHAPTER 2
SOCIAL ANXIETY

Social anxiety is a catch-all phrase for the dread, uncertainty, and worry that most individuals experience from time to time in their interactions with others.

Individuals with social anxiety claim to be shy and may have been shy their whole lives, while some individuals who are not shy also struggle with social anxiety. Individuals face social anxiety when they believe they will do something mortifying or disappointing.

Social anxiety makes you think that other individuals are evaluating you negatively because of anything you said or did. The dread of doing anything embarrassing or humiliating is restricting. It also makes one feel self-conscious and aware of the likelihood that one may do something embarrassing or humiliating.

Who would want to engage in conversation if they knew it would only disclose their awkwardness, inadequacies, or inclination to blush? Socially anxious people often believe that their encounters with others will be excruciatingly revealing. Others will see their flaws or discomfort and reject, ignore, criticize, or dismiss them for not acting more acceptably (Stein, 2008).

When you see things this way, it's tough to communicate naturally with others, and it's difficult to chat, listen, or form friends. It frequently leads to isolation and loneliness. For many individuals, one of the most heart-breaking aspects of having this disease is that it stops them from being intimate with others or finding a partner with whom to spend their lives.

Socially anxious individuals are frequently friendly to others and have a fair share of the good attributes that others value. They may have a sense of humor, be active and kind, generous and understanding, serious, humorous, quiet, or vivacious, and they act in various ways naturally when they are at ease.

However, because feeling at ease in company is difficult for the socially anxious and causes them anxiety, these attributes are frequently hidden from view. Their fear hampers their capacity to communicate themselves, and their ability (Stein, 2008) to do so may have been rusty due to lack of use. Indeed, socially apprehensive individuals may have lost faith in their appealing traits and self-confidence.

One of the benefits of learning to manage social anxiety is that it helps you express previously inhibited elements of yourself, allowing you to appreciate – rather than dread – being yourself. Finally, it teaches you to trust yourself rather than mistrust yourself since you realize that no one's social behavior is faultless and everyone makes errors. Mistakes are acceptable; they are a natural part of being human, and there is no need to let them derail you.

IDENTIFYING THE ISSUE

Definitions are essential because they help us focus on the aspects of social anxiety caused by ADHD that create discomfort and prolong the anguish.

Anxiety about social situations is common. Everyone experiences it at some point (so everyone understands it). It would be insane for us to believe that we would never experience social anxiety again. Seeking a complete cure would be trying the impossible. Instead, it is beneficial to begin by defining when social anxiety becomes an issue if you have ADHD and then understand the factors that contribute to it persisting.

As you'll see in the next chapters, concentrating your efforts on improving these things – particularly learning how to be less self-conscious – may make a tremendous impact. It alleviates pain and suffering and allows you to live the life you want. But first, you must comprehend the concept of social anxiety.

The American Psychiatric Association's Diagnostic and Statistical Manual (Stein, 2008) defines the type and level of social anxiety that qualifies someone for a diagnosis of social anxiety related to ADHD. The guidebook outlines four major criteria:

1. Persistent apprehension about one or more social or performance circumstances in which the individual is exposed to new individuals or may be scrutinized by others. The individual is afraid that they would act unpleasant and humiliatingly (or exhibit anxiety symptoms). It is important to note that individuals with social phobia may not do something humiliating or unpleasant; they only fear that they will. Their symptoms don't even have to be visible. They merely need to consider the prospect of something happening to become afraid and nervous.

2. Exposure to dreaded social settings nearly always causes anxiety, like talking on the phone, approaching a crowded room, or speaking publicly in front of others. While there is not a hard and fast distinction between normal and clinical anxiety levels, there are various levels of social anxiety.

3. The individual knows that their dread is unwarranted or excessive. One of the most problematic aspects of having social anxiety disorder due to ADHD is knowing that what makes you worry is not harmful and may not affect other people. But understanding that you suffer "irrationally" and "excessively" in comparison to others and that your pain is in some ways unwarranted simply makes it worse. It might leave you feeling insecure, nervous, incompetent, or inferior.

4. Fearful circumstances are avoided or endured with great worry or pain. It's only natural to avoid or flee from terrifying circumstances. The sensation of terror warns you of the probability of danger, and staying might be dangerous. On the other hand, people who suffer from social anxiety are tough since they do not want to be isolated and lonely. They have no control over the origins of their fear. Interaction with others – such as shopping, traveling, or working – cannot be avoided entirely. Socially anxious individuals, like everyone else, want to work, make friends, and feel like they belong. Rather than avoiding or fleeing tough situations, people may tolerate these stressful situations despite their misery, focusing on keeping the dangers or hazards as low as possible and keeping themselves as secure as possible. Because of the severity of their worry, this technique appears only logical.

Whether or not these features of the condition are severe enough to meet diagnostic criteria is, to some part, a question of professional judgment, as there is no hard and fast rule for determining what level of suffering counts as substantial. Dreading public speaking is the most prevalent fear mentioned by individuals with social anxiety disorder caused by ADHD (75% of people with this diagnosis are terrified to speak in public). However, one of the most commonly listed anxieties is the fear of public speaking. It is, in fact, more frequent than the fear of death.

Social anxiety can be divided into two types (Stein, 2008). For some, social anxiety is restricted to a few settings, such as dining in public or being among sexually attractive individuals; for others, it is more likely to influence most scenarios requiring interaction.

Because there is no clear and fast line between being socially anxious and having a medically diagnosable disease, this book will use the everyday usage of social anxiety rather than 'social anxiety due to ADHD.'

THE CONNECTION BETWEEN ADHD AND SOCIAL ANXIETY

It's important to realize that ADHD affects many individuals — around 4.4 percent (Rodebaugh, Heimberg & Holaway, 2004) of American adults and up to 10% of American adults children. The same is true for social anxiety, which affects an average of 12.1% of Americans at some point in their lives.

Social anxiety is a mental health diagnosis characterized by worry or anxiety about social circumstances in which others may scrutinize the individual. Typically, the individual is terrified of acting in a humiliating or unpleasant manner, which would result in rejection. Individuals with social anxiety virtually always experience discomfort in social interactions, and they frequently avoid social events entirely due to worry or pain.

According to the CDC, children with ADHD are more likely to have additional mental health issues such as anxiety, stress, depression, and autism spectrum disorder, making social connections more challenging.

The CDC also reports that approximately one in every ten children with ADHD has anxiety. According to a 2015 study, there is a relationship between social anxiety and ADHD. Anxiety and ADHD are typical co-occurring disorders, and social anxiety and ADHD are not rare.

When people are uneasy or anxious in social situations, they may want to touch items or fidget with their fingers. This uneasiness in social situations is also frequent among people with ADHD. Once they are required to concentrate or sit still, they may fidget.

ADHD never travels alone, and social anxiety is a familiar companion. Social anxiety may severely hinder professional and academic performance and relationships, whether you can't consume food around others, avoid cafés or stores due to stranger discussions, or despise public speaking.

Many ADHD teenagers and young adults have social anxiety due to executive functioning issues with emotional regulation, learning and memory, and self-awareness. People who suffer from social anxiety may avoid specific triggering scenarios such as in-person classes, while others may feel extremely uneasy and awkward in any social setting (Rodebaugh, Heimberg & Holaway, 2004).

An intense dread causes social anxiety that others criticize you so harshly that their replies will crush you. When you are preoccupied with the negative judgments of others, you are unable to be yourself, form great connections, or construct a fulfilling life. Instead, social anxiety stymies you at every turn.

ADHD | SOCIAL ANXIETY

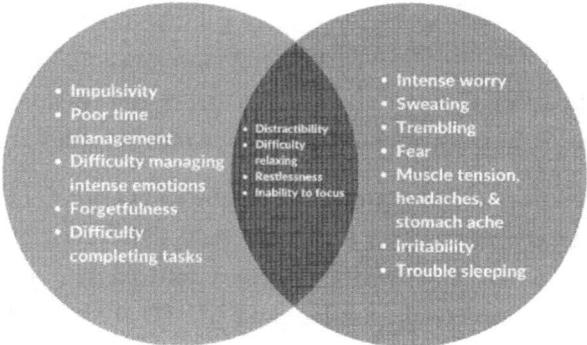

- Impulsivity
- Poor time management
- Difficulty managing intense emotions
- Forgetfulness
- Difficulty completing tasks

- Distractibility
- Difficulty relaxing
- Restlessness
- Inability to focus

- Intense worry
- Sweating
- Trembling
- Fear
- Muscle tension, headaches, & stomach ache
- Irritability
- Trouble sleeping

(Cuncic, 2021)

THE SIGNS AND SYMPTOMS OF SOCIAL ANXIETY

The Venn Diagram describes the four major categories of ADHD and social anxiety. No two individuals are the same, and there are several possible symptoms, so if the ones you are experiencing are not present, simply add them to the list (Rodebaugh, Heimberg & Holaway, 2004).

To begin assessing the problem for yourself, consider how your interpretation of social anxiety impacts your thoughts, behaviors, body, and emotions. It would be odd not to have any symptoms in any of these four different categories, but some of them might be difficult to recognize at first. Spend some time thinking about your specific experience with social anxiety, using this list as a suggestion.

Effects on thoughts

• Concerning yourself with what others think of you.

• Difficulty concentrating or remembering what others say.

• Concentrating your focus on yourself and being very aware of what you do and say.

• Considering what may go wrong ahead of time.

• Ruminating about an event after it already happened to examine if you did anything wrong.

Effects on behavior

• Speaking fast or silently, muttering, or mispronouncing words.

• Avoid seeing someone by taking precautions to ensure that you do not draw attention to yourself.

• Keeping safe by avoiding awkward social circumstances or scenarios.

Physical effects

• Anxiety symptoms visible to others, such as flushing, sweating, or shaking.

• Tension: the aches and pains that come from not being able to relax.

• Panic attacks: hammering heart, dizziness or nausea, or shortness of breath.

Effects on emotions

• Anxiety, fear, apprehension, and self-consciousness.

• Frustration and rage directed towards oneself or others.

• Feelings of inadequacy and lack of confidence.

• Feeling down, dejected, or despairing about your ability to change.

In practice, the symptoms interact in diverse ways, such that ideas, behaviors, physiological reactions, and emotions (or feelings) all impact one another. For example, believing you look silly makes you feel self-conscious, so you turn aside and attempt to blend into the background, which causes you to become aware that you are shivering and your heart is pounding. Or, since you're sweaty and panicked, it's challenging to think of what to say, so you blurt out something that makes no sense, and then you feel ashamed.

HOW DOES IT FEEL TO HAVE THIS PROBLEM?

A description and a list of symptoms are good places to start when thinking about social anxiety, but they don't give the whole picture or explain the pain involved. It is not unexpected that a disease that can touch many facets of life should have far-reaching consequences.

SUBTLE KINDS OF AVOIDANCE

While some socially anxious individuals avoid going out with friends, attending meetings, or attending social occasions like weddings, others continue to attend events they fear. This participation gives the impression that they are not fearful of these situations, but this ignores the numerous subtle ways one might avoid disagreeable circumstances, such as speaking gently or hurrying on. It is critical not to ignore subtle forms of avoidance since they play a significant role in perpetuating the issue like other forms of avoidance. Below are a few more examples.

Subtle kinds of avoidance examples

• Waiting for somebody else to arrive before entering a crowded room.

• Putting things off, such as visiting the neighbours or shopping during peak hours.

• Turning aside when you notice someone is approaching who makes you nervous.

• Refusing to discuss anything personal.

• Not using your hands if you believe that people are looking.

• Refusing to eat in public places.

BEHAVIORS THAT PROMOTE SAFETY

Other people are a source of anxiety for those who are socially anxious, and one of the issues with other people is that you never know what they will do next. They may, unwittingly, touch you at any time, make you feel weird by asking you a specific question, introduce you to someone who makes you feel most anxious, ask for your viewpoint, or simply walk away from you to speak to someone else. When you're with other people, you can feel constantly threatened, and it's not easy to figure out what you should do to stop feeling bad. In these scenarios, your mind instinctively shifts to thinking about how to be safe.

Socially anxious people create safety behaviors or things they do to decrease their sense of being at risk, such as looking at the floor to avoid eye contact, wearing make-up to conceal their blushes, or leaving the room as soon as a meeting is over, so they don't have to engage in small talk. Below are some more instances of safe practices.

As you read through the list below, you will see that some of them appear to be opposed – such as being silent or attempting to continue the discussion – but this is because different people desire to do various things to feel safe.

Some people feel comfortable saying little and making sure that what they say makes sense. These behaviors give them the impression that they are less likely to make a fool of themselves. Some feel safer if they take charge of keeping a discussion going. It might feel safer to keep talking when quiet feels like an eternity, even if you're not making any sense.

Safety behavior* examples

• Rehearse what you're about to say and mentally double-check that you've got the words correct.

• Speaking slowly or softly or speaking quickly and not pausing to take a breath.

• Putting your hands to your mouth or hiding your hands or face.

• Tightening your grip or locking your knees together to control shaking.

• Allowing your hair to fall in front of your face, wearing loose-fitting clothing, attempting to amuse others by telling jokes, or never risking telling a joke.

• Not talking about yourself or your thoughts; refraining from expressing your ideas.

• Saying nothing that may be construed as challenging or contentious; always agreeing with others.

• Wearing clothing that will allow you to blend in.

• Keeping close to a safe person or in a safe location; not taking any chances.

• Looking for the exit route whenever you are out in public.

Safety behavior is anything you do to keep yourself safe. Many safety behaviors entail avoiding unwanted attention.

DWELLING ON THE ISSUE

Social anxiety may strike at any time and can feel overpowering, partially because of the uncertainty of others and partly because the dread of it is continually in mind. Anticipating worry contributes to the problem. When I think about future meetings, I think about how things may go wrong, typically in mysterious and terrifying ways.

Even after an incident, the mind remains vulnerable to increased worry by repeatedly replaying ideas, pictures, and recollections of what occurred. Socially anxious people tend to fixate on parts of their relationships with others that bother them. People who suffer from social anxiety perform post-mortems based on what they believe happened rather than what actually occurred, on what they believe other people thought of them rather than what they actually thought.

SELF-ESTEEM, SELF-CONFIDENCE, AND INFERIORITY FEELINGS

Social anxiety provokes different negative reactions and actions. Often you feel as if you are less promising than others or more strange, which affects your self-esteem and self-confidence.

You start to expect people to reject or ignore you, and you interpret their actions – such as the way they look at you or talk to you – as signals that they dislike you. You are afraid of becoming the target of their criticism or unfavorable appraisal or of being found wanting in some manner as if someone will expose your flaws or deficiencies.

As a result, you may have a persistent undertone of terror, as if you are lurching from one lucky escape to the next. Some socially anxious individuals believe that if others knew what they were truly like, they would abandon them altogether. Social anxious individuals will go to extraordinary measures to disguise their "true selves" even if nothing is problematic with them other than feeling nervous.

Of course, this makes it difficult for them to convey an opinion or communicate how they feel about something. They may also believe that other individuals are never socially anxious, that they have less – or less socially revealing – flaws and shortcomings, or that they can go through life without worrying about what others think of them. In reality, being impervious to others produces just as many issues as being too sensitive to them.

FRUSTRATION AND ANGER; DEMORALIZATION AND SADNESS

It feels difficult to suppress elements of your character, so it's no surprise that social anxiety may depress you after a time. When it conflicts with doing the things you want to do and being the kind of person you want to be, knowing you can be around people brings a slew of other emotions. You may feel demoralized, sad, nervous, bitter, and frustrated that others seem to find so many things simple that you find difficult. Anxiety is not the sole emotion linked to social anxiety.

PERFORMANCE CONSEQUENCES

The problem with excessive anxiety levels is that they disrupt activities and the capacity to carry out plans. They make it more difficult for individuals to perform to the best of their ability and impede them from accomplishing their goals. A certain amount of worry is beneficial if you have to go to an interview or take an exam as it may energize and encourage you and help you concentrate your attention. Too much anxiety, however, becomes a distraction and makes it difficult to act normally or do your best. This anxiety might also make it difficult for people to know you. Social anxiety prevents individuals from doing what they desire and are capable of accomplishing. This may have a wide variety of diverse implications on professions, personal relationships, friendships, jobs, and leisure activities in the long term.

The following illustrates how social anxiety can affect someone:

(Cuncic, 2021)

Social anxiety may be restricted to one significant life element– such as eating or speaking in public – but it is more often associated with broader and more widespread impacts. Some individuals do well at work until they are promoted to a position that requires them to be more "visible" or supervise others. They may be unable to accept the promotion because it requires them to attend meetings where they must account for their department's operations or give presentations, attend a training program, or organize, monitor, and assume responsibility for the work of others. These individuals may decline advancement and stay in professions well below their talents, so they fail to realize a large portion of their potential.

Others may function effectively at work – even in high-profile profes-sional occupations or socially demanding – such as sales or public relations. These individuals have few issues as long as workplace customs shelter them. They are okay in the lab, computer room, or operation theatre, but they may feel lost in unplanned social events or when their position is not clearly defined. They find it difficult to establish acquaintances and have a hard time making small talk (Koyuncu, Ertekin, Yüksel, Aslantaş, Ertekin, Çelebi, Binbay & Tükel, 2015). Despite their professional success, they may still feel isolated and lonely, and their social anxiety may cause them to miss out on chances to build deep and personal connections.

Many people suffer from what is known as dating anxiety. This anxiety is common enough to be considered entirely normal, and people go through these agonies when they find someone good-looking. They cannot do the things that will help them get to know the person they feel strongly about.

Others have one or two close friends and feel most at ease in the company of individuals they know well, like when they are with their spouses or encircled by their family. Social anxiety makes it difficult for them to meet new people, move to new areas, or find new methods to please themselves, and their lives may become severely confined and constricted.

CHAPTER 3
ADHD AND SOCIAL ANXIETY
THE ENDLESS CONNECTION

Anxiety is a common disorder in the general population, but it is more prevalent in those with ADHD. Their comorbidity rates are estimated to be approximately 25%. Nonetheless, these figures imply that most people with ADHD do not have accompanying anxiety issues, but this is not our clinical opinion.

Studies often use strict cut-offs that put a person in or out of a certain group. These studies are useful in identifying people who have a comorbid anxiety disorder with a degree of functional impairment. Nevertheless, many people may not legally satisfy a type of disease. Still, they arrive with anxiety issues, which generally arise (Koyuncu, Ertekin, Yüksel, Aslantaş, Ertekin, Çelebi, Binbay & Tükel, 2015) from previous experience and a lack of confidence, which may impede their progress in therapy.

ADHD and anxiety comorbidity rates are associated with the similarities between ADHD and anxiety symptoms (restlessness, lack of attention, unceasing mental activity). Furthermore, a 25% overlap has been documented in community and clinic research, indicating that comorbidity rates are unlikely to merely reflect symptoms being 'counted' twice in around one-quarter of cases.

Anxiety is described as a side effect of stimulant medications in certain circumstances. When this occurs after treatment, it may be beneficial to urge a mental assessment and potential switch to non-stimulant medication.

Perinatal issues – such as late pregnancy difficulties, problems after birth, and the neonatal period – have been identified as risk factors for comorbid ADHD and anxiety, especially in individuals without a family history of ADHD. Consequently, many people enter the world predisposed to develop nervous and maladaptive coping techniques.

These maladaptive coping techniques manifest because of repeated criticism from others (both actual and imagined), which causes people to be frightened about completing activities or entering settings. Adults with ADHD may develop "anticipatory anxiety" about circumstances in which they have previously encountered disappointment and/or failure due to disadvantages in academic success, failure in the job, and difficulties getting along with others.

People with anxiety and ADHD may become fixated with their previous behaviors and/or performance and worry about future occurrences and interpersonal performance. Individuals may relive unpleasant memories, such as when they think they have done poorly, when they believe others have assessed them to be 'below standard' compared to others, and moments of shame due to mistakes of judgment and/or improper behavior.

Anxiety is likely to manifest itself in various ways in ADHD adults. People with ADHD are more prone to be self-conscious or vulnerable to shame or humiliation.

Most individuals with ADHD experience anxiety in school as 'performance anxiety,' such as when they have to get up in class and read aloud. They make typos, misspell words, and sometimes skip whole sentences. Their classmates ridicule or bully them or mock and call them names. In such circumstances, people may retreat or rashly strike out. In any case, this has a detrimental social impact, and ADHD young adults lose their capacity to engage comfortably with their classmates (Koyuncu, Ertekin, Yüksel, Aslantaş, Ertekin, Çelebi, Binbay & Tükel, 2015).

Some young adults overcompensate by striving to satisfy everyone or bullying other kids. Others make up for it by being the class clown. They may seek friendships at school from children outside of their peer group or prefer adult company.

Small fears grow into larger anxieties over time, compounded as individuals go from school into early adulthood and face higher scholastic and social obligations. The early nervous ADHD kid has evolved a method of interacting with the environment built on uncertainty and uneasiness before they even know where they are. Anxiety becomes widespread, undermining their views and confidence in their ability to succeed in almost whatever they undertake. This anxiety sometimes leads to a preoccupation or over-concern about their ability to perform numerous jobs and areas of function.

In today's culture, a person's work, home, or car they drive symbolizes their success. There are several expectations to meet, necessitating the capacity to multitask and take on different duties and positions. Whether your title is mother, father, wife, spouse, daughter, son, friend, church member, youth leader, advisor, manager, worker, or executive, you must juggle these positions and your other responsibilities. It might seem like there are many plates spinning in the air. Society is fast and hectic, and individuals with ADHD prefer speed above precision, so when they work quickly, they make mistakes and fail.

Everything else one needs to think about or accomplish becomes considerably more difficult when one is worried. Anxiety influences cognitive processes by influencing the assessment and evaluation of events, resulting in an internal shift of emphasis to excessive self-monitoring and self-regulation.

Anxiety worsens attention problems and impulsivity. It may impair one's capacity to reason. As a result, ADHD people – who already have cognitive weaknesses – will become even more susceptible to anxious circumstances by functioning less effectively. For someone with generalised anxiety disorder, this means they get a "double dosage" of cognitive impairments since ADHD symptoms become much more prominent when they need to concentrate the most. This anxiety makes ADHD evaluation more difficult since these individuals get agitated at the testing site.

Many cognitive tests begin with straightforward tasks and grow progressively more difficult to measure individual variations in strengths and limitations. This increase in difficulty implies that a person will inevitably reach a point when they cannot answer a question or solve a puzzle.

This testing technique may confirm existing notions that they are "stupid" or may have them relive terrible school memories. Individuals who get very worried are less likely to perform effectively and are more likely to abandon assignments, leading them to fall short of their potential and the tester to underestimate their level of performance. Children with comorbid anxiety and ADHD perform worse on activities requiring short-term or working memory, i.e., tasks requiring both active processing and transitory information storage.

Anxiety may redirect resources away from storage and processing within the working memory system. However, it is theorized that anxiety serves a motivating purpose by increasing arousal, which may enhance attentional control. This increased arousal is more likely to happen in activities that do not need knowledge retention (i.e., memory processing) but require the person to block a response, such as continuous performance or stop tasks. Children with ADHD and accompanying anxiety may do better in such activities. Unfortunately, there has not been any research on people with comorbid ADHD and anxiety.

Anxiety disorders may manifest themselves in various ways, including generalised anxiety, social phobia, simple phobia, phobias, panic disorder, obsessive-compulsive disorder, and post-traumatic stress disorder. Individuals with ADHD are more likely to have generalised anxiety, but individuals (Koyuncu, Ertekin, Yüksel, Aslantaş, Ertekin, Çelebi, Binbay

& Tükel, 2015) have also reported social phobia, panic disorder, and obsessive-compulsive disorder.

These are not mutually exclusive categories, and ADHD adults may have difficulties. Difficulties may be more visible depending on the social, academic, or vocational obligations, as well as their life history at the moment (Koyuncu, Ertekin, Yüksel, Aslantaş, Ertekin, Çelebi, Binbay & Tükel, 2015). For example, depending on the scenario, a person may have generalised anxiety difficulties and social phobia, and in times of extreme stress, they may also suffer panic symptoms.

People with ADHD may develop social anxiety subsequently to their overall concern about everything and everyone they meet. Feeling different from their peers causes some people to compare themselves to others on a frequent and unfavourable basis, resulting in them selectively responding to their own perceived bad attributes and the good characteristics of others.

Some individuals may regularly need reassurance in social settings, such as "Did I come across okay?" or "Was I not diplomatic?" They feel self-conscious and awkward because they are concerned that others are watching them in social situations. Some individuals attempt to compensate by behaving foolishly and becoming the "heart and soul of the party." In such cases, anxiety treatments should aim to reduce anxious thoughts, feelings, and behavior and calm the individual so that they do not respond in an overly excited manner. This calming allows the person to avoid drawing undue attention to themselves by behaving in a bizarre and/or inappropriate manner (which others may perceive as childish). This is not to reduce individuals with ADHD's innate inventiveness and passion but to urge the individual to act with greater control and maturity.

Because the incidence of ADHD is greater among people with Tourette's syndrome and the rate of Tourette's is higher among those with ADHD, the increased prevalence of the obsessive-compulsive disorder in those with ADHD may be mediated by its linkages with Tourette's syndrome. Obsessive Compulsive Disorder (OCD) symptoms are also likely to exacerbate attention problems by shifting available resources to obsessive thoughts.

Symptoms connected with OCD, on the other hand, may be tactics adopted by individuals with ADHD to compensate for an attention deficit by checking for mistakes or items they may have forgotten. However, when a person's anxiety level rises, this checking behavior may become more repetitive and compulsive (Koyuncu, Ertekin, Yüksel, Aslantaş, Ertekin, Çelebi, Binbay & Tükel, 2015). Individuals may be embarrassed by their private obsessions or compulsions, which may prompt them to avoid discussing them with doctors, especially during their evaluation. They may believe that by treating their ADHD, their OCD symptoms will go away.

Over-focusing in an obsessive or perseverative manner may lead to task failure owing to excessive concentration on a small part of a job. Some people who struggle with these issues may choose not to undertake a job rather than risk doing it badly. Exploration and questioning concepts and rigorous desensitization are effective therapy techniques for reducing repetitive checking behaviors.

Because ADHD symptoms and anxiety symptoms overlap, it is critical to conduct a thorough and comprehensive evaluation of the anxiety-related problem and determine the relationship between the individual's thoughts, beliefs, feelings, and behaviors regarding their ability to complete a task or perform competently in a situation. As with standard cognitive behavioral anxiety therapy, a psychoeducational component explaining the anxiety model and the link between cognition and behavior is essential.

ASSESSMENT

Before we jump onto possible solutions, let's look at this questionnaire.

Check how often you have experienced the following symptoms:

General Anxiety	Never	Occasionally	Sometimes	Often	Very Often	Always
I have worried about money, paying bills, and debts.						
I have worried about not being able to finish work/ tasks/ school assignments.						
I am worried about my health.						
I am worried about the future and things going wrong.						
I am worried that I have failed as a parent/ employee/ son/ daughter.						

Social Anxiety	Never	Occasionally	Sometimes	Often	Very Often	Always
I am self-conscious.						
I avoid social events.						
I avoid crowds.						
I am worried about performance.						
I am worried about meeting other people.						

Panic	Never	Occasionally	Sometimes	Often	Very Often	Always
I have felt a constriction in my chest.						
I have felt heart palpitations.						
I thought I was having a heart attack.						
I felt dizzy, and I fainted.						
I feel the blood rushing around my head.						

Obsessive-compulsive disorder	Never	Occasionally	Sometimes	Often	Very Often	Always
I felt uncomfortable if the house was not tidy or clean.						
I need to check everything several times.						
I have to do things in a routine; otherwise, I become worried.						
I tend to over-focus.						
I had intrusive thoughts.						

The anxiety checklist is introduced above and crafted around concepts frequently discussed as a cause of anxiety by individuals at clinics (generalized anxiety, social anxiety, panic, obsessive-compulsive issues) to assist the client and therapist in identifying the subtype of the comorbid presenting problem of anxiety.

Thus, the anxiety checklist (Koyuncu, Ertekin, Yüksel, Aslantaş, Ertekin, Çelebi, Binbay & Tükel, 2015) serves as a helpful guide for determining whether anxiety problems are general or specific. It also serves as a foundation for conversation and exploration, allowing you to take an adaptive treatment approach and fundamentally plan and structure treatment. However, anxiety classifications are not mutually exclusive.

TREATMENT

When treating people with ADHD and chronic anxiety vs. treating individuals without ADHD who have anxiety, there are two major differences:

1. Recognize the overlap in anxiety and ADHD symptoms and try to separate the best treatment symptoms by the approaches recommended in the following chapters to improve attention and decrease impulsivity.

2. Because ADHD people have trouble deferring pleasure, it is critical to implement an instant reward system to positively reinforce success and performance on a much more regular basis than is now used.

The suggested treatment models are based on critical steps of the therapy process: cognitive behavioral psychoeducation on the anxiety model, learning to deal with negative thoughts, developing self-control, and modifying behavior.

CHAPTER 4
WHAT DO YOU HAVE TO DO?

We discussed the current concept of Attention-Deficit/Hyperactivity Disorder (ADHD) as an issue connected to executive function or motivational deficiencies in Chapter 1. Executive functions constitute the self-regulation that enables you to select and complete activities across time to attain personally meaningful goals.

The problem for most individuals with ADHD is not a lack of objectives or desire, but rather that ADHD interferes with the constant follow-through on the stage process procedure over time to attain those goals, particularly when the result does not (Çelebi & Ünal, 2021) come quickly enough. For instance, we all want to be in better physical condition, but it may be tough to stick to a daily regimen of eating healthier and exercising until we get the desired effects.

Adults with ADHD find it even more challenging to break down long-term or significant objectives into step-by-step strategies and then continuously implement these plans. To that aim, it is essential to establish precise and explicit plans throughout the day.

These intentions aid in the organisation and movement of your day. This is especially true on days (such as the weekend) or periods of the day when you lack the structure offered by your job, school, or other regular responsibilities. You may be self-employed, a graduate student focusing on a thesis, or a stay-at-home parent, all of which require you to create your own schedule to a considerable extent. The fourth chapter will go through how to use a daily planner to organize and arrange your schedule. For the time being, your responsibility is to define the exact activities you will complete on a given day that, when combined, will build the structure for your day.

Task selection and prioritising, and providing a framework for your day represent how you choose to "spend yourself," including your commitment of time, energy, and effort. There will be a plethora of tasks to sift through, including somewhat basic domestic duties (taking out the trash), vital errands and tasks (grocery shopping, paying bills), leisure, cultivating connections, and other important personal pursuits (exercise, work, school).

This chapter aims to explore the to-do list as a tool for identifying, sorting through, and prioritising the numerous necessary chores and activities in your life. To make the to-do list manageable and functional, we will distinguish between complete and daily to-do lists and talk about how to prioritize and increase the chances of completing chores. The first stage in the process is to make a plan and schedule time to do so.

TIME FOR PLANNING

Although we are just getting started with the concept of "having time to plan," it will be a recurring problem for managing time and other coping skills throughout this book. Planning is a commitment that needs an initial commitment of time and effort—often much less than you expect —for higher profits later in the day, week, and month—often much more than you wish.

Living with ADHD and anxiety involves time and effort, which is inevitable. Most individuals with ADHD and anxiety believe that others do not have to go through all these processes to manage their day. This viewpoint may provoke a long-held feeling of being different from others or act as a justification for not devoting time and effort to working on a to-do list which can be perceived as "unnatural" or "strange." Because of this feeling, you resist making an effort to start a to-do list and tell yourself that you'll be able to handle all your daily tasks without a to-do list. Sadly, frequently failing to plan results in the feeling that you do not achieve anything meaningful at the end of the day.

In reality, most non-ADHD and anxiety individuals organize (Çelebi & Ünal, 2021) their days and utilize some version of a to-do list. Someone who does not have ADHD and anxiety may be able to avoid writing down or going back to their work lists, and their follow-through looks to be easy. These people have most likely established habits that need less effort to maintain, but everyone spends some time and effort organising their day.

This book suggests devoting an "honest" 10 minutes to working on the planning activities outlined below in terms of what to accomplish. Working on the to-do list requires just an electronic word processing file or worksheet, a smartphone's notepad function, or simply (and arguably the best approach) paper and pen.

The more clear and definite your strategy for planning, the better. We recommend that you designate a particular location where you will sit to work on your to-do list at a realistic time of the day or when you will have at least 10 minutes to dedicate to it. Adults with ADHD and anxiety may express being distracted by other ideas or having difficulties concentrating at first, so we recommend a 600-second time commitment—the "honest" 10 minutes – until planning becomes a habit. This time range allows you to participate in and finish the activity and "remember to remember" what you need to accomplish.

The previous phases are designed to put you in a position to create your strategy. You should strive to use the same location each day at the same time to spend your 10 minutes planning (Hallowell, 2022). The concept may be modified to the situation, especially if you cannot use the same location to plan your to-do list.

To prioritize and create a list of things to do on a given day, you must first comprehend the many duties, responsibilities, and commitments that supply you with a laundry list of possibilities. The next section covers the function of the complete to-do list.

You must:

1. Devote 600 seconds or 10 minutes to planning.

2. Find an area free of distractions.

3. Plan your day for 10 minutes (600 seconds).

4. Make a note of your intentions in your daily planner.

5. Define to-do items using strong, behavioral phrases for what you want to "do."

A COMPLETE TO-DO LIST

The complete to-do list is what its name implies: a complete list of your many activities, obligations, and projects. It is also known as a "dump list" of everything required. The attempt to remember multiple responsibilities throughout the day, with several extra ones "popping into mind" at inconvenient times (Hallowell, 2022), such as the awful, too-late recollection of things forgotten ("Oh no, my friend's birthday was yesterday and I forgot it!"), as well as those foreboding issues that randomly pop up but are not yet urgent ("Valentine's Day falls on a Friday; I should make dinner arrangements sooner rather than later.").

Instead of attempting to remember everything, the complete to-do list is an externalized and customized record of everything you need to do. The list serves two purposes: first, to provide a method for thinking through and unloading these duties, and second, to provide a lasting record of them so that you do not have to recall and keep the list in your thoughts constantly.

Based on your specific situation, you will decide how "complete" you want your list to be. For the most part, your complete list will span the next one to six weeks, with things about the next week taking precedence on your daily list. However, there may be approaching events that demand immediate attention, such as holiday plans, business travels, or school or work assignments that cannot be put off until the last minute.

It is also helpful to think through some activities that do not have a time-frame but are characterised as tasks to be completed shortly or other activities that are currently low priority but will become important in the future.

"It is too daunting for me to think about and confront all I have to accomplish every day" is a frequent response to the concept of the complete to-do list. We understand that it is daunting, so you should get it out of your mind, write it down, and store it for future reference. The complete to-do list allows you to write down and organize these random activities and thoughts, so you do not forget to complete an essential task.

The complete to-do list should be reviewed regularly to help you recall and identify priorities and integrate new activities and commitments that may have emerged since the last review. You are not expected to create a new to-do list every day; rather, this is an exercise to help you focus on your most critical short-, mid-, and long-term chores over the next six weeks or so. However, many people find it beneficial to sit down at times to review and update their lists or spend some time starting a new to-do list to get a grip on what needs to be done in the coming several weeks.

You must:

1. Get a notebook or open a word document to keep track of your complete to-do list.

2. Find an area free of distractions.

3. Make a list of your duties, plans, chores, commitments, leisure ideas, and so on for the next one to six weeks (or whatever period works best for you). This list is your "dump list."

4. Keep your notebook or word document close to you.

5. The complete to-do list reminds you of activities and responsibilities without depending on your memory. Refer to it regularly for useful reminders of things you can accomplish, but this is not your daily to-do list.

DAILY TO-DO LIST

The daily to-do list – as the name suggests – is a daily list that provides a personalised collection of activity reminders that are important to you. You don't need a reminder to get to work, but you will need to make a particular business-related phone call or dedicate time to a report throughout your workday.

To-do activities are duties that demand a concentrated effort from you to complete throughout the length of a regular day, such as shopping, booking a medical appointment, meditating, or doing a specific household activity (such as unloading the dishwasher). You can use this list to specify particular responsibilities in various jobs.

The point of the list is to record all your outstanding duties, while the daily to-do list is intended to be an easy-to-access, disposable list of activities for today. We recommend writing the list on a little index card that may be kept in your pocket or other easily accessible position (like posted on a computer display or other conspicuous location).

The modest size of the note card should keep the work list reasonable, with our advice being to start with two or three activities (and certainly no more than five) to prevent feeling overwhelmed. Phones and other electrical gadgets include notepad functions that are simple and helpful. An old-fashioned paper version is still a faster and simpler method to retrieve and refresh your memory (Hallowell, 2022). Writing down the list by hand boosts task encoding and prepares you for behavioral follow-through. In any case, you must choose a simple format to use and manage.

Another general rule for creating the daily to-do list is to specify tasks in precise, behavioral terms to maximise the chance of completion. For instance, you may have a list item that reads "clean up the kitchen." Even though this is a personally meaningful chore, when phrased as such, it becomes too daunting since it includes multiple smaller tasks (empty dishwasher, load dishwasher, wash down counters, clean inside of the microwave, arrange cabinets, and so on). You may not know where to begin, which increases tension, and finally allows you to postpone the chore, generally with a comfortable but ultimately self-defeating justification like "I'll check my email, and then I'll be in the mood to fix the kitchen."

The ability to split enormous tasks into components is an important coping skill mentioned in subsequent chapters. This talent is not a surprise to anybody with ADHD and anxiety, but this list allows you to put it into practice in precise ways. As previously shown, "clean up the kitchen" may be more clearly and behaviorally defined as "load dishwasher and place clean dishes where they go," or whatever starting action seems achievable to you at the time ("I will empty the bowls").

It's okay if you finish that work and opt not to do anything else. You may add another kitchen-related job to your daily to-do list for the following day. On the other hand, most individuals with ADHD and anxiety have observed that once they get started, they generally stay moving" and will add additional tasks to their list.

The first precise and behaviorally defined activity is meant to stimulate and engage you by making the first step reasonable, similar to wading into the shallow end of a swimming pool. This first step gets you started, and you'll probably wind up doing more than you expected since the work isn't as awful as you thought it would be.

CONSTRUCT A STRATEGY

Making a daily to-do list and checking it throughout the day can help you stay on top of these priorities. Each review and reminder exposes you to something you would normally avoid and prepares you for action rather than allowing these vital chores to fall victim to poor recall or engagement in diversions.

The reminder to enter the room with a strategy is a good motto to keep your priorities front and center while performing your tasks. One of the difficulties of ADHD and anxiety are resisting the want to do something more exciting but less significant than what you set out to achieve.

Entering a room with a strategy requires reminding oneself of the purpose of entering the room, storing or accessing a computer file, or doing any other activity included in your immediate task plan. When you obtain something for a project or transition between chores, you are open to distraction.

Entering the room with a strategy provides you with a goal to strive toward, such as not clicking on the Internet icon while opening a computer file for a work assignment ("I am going to work on the report until 2 pm, and then I can start playing games.")

This coping mechanism may also assist you in returning to a task when you find yourself wandering at home or work when you want to be productive ("I came downstairs to grab paper for the printer. I'll collect it and return upstairs to continue my job").

It is critical to anticipate typical triggers for distraction and flight from work and devise proactive strategies to cope with them.

You must:

Daily To-Do List

1. Locate a piece of paper, the back of an invoice, or another piece of throwaway paper.

2. Devote ten minutes to creating your daily to-do list.

3. Your daily to-do list consists of tasks that are not on your regular schedule but demand a particular commitment of time and effort.

4. Keep your list to a maximum of two to five things. When in doubt, go on the side of fewer things rather than more—you can always add more after you finish them.

5. Specify tasks in behavioral terms or acts you can "do."

6. Determine a reasonable time period for completing each activity.

7. Use your daily planner to identify periods throughout the day when you will "appoint" yourself to do each assignment.

8. Complete each assignment on time and cross it off the list.

Enter the Room with a Strategy

1. Explain why you're entering a room (or workplace, sitting at a desk, etc.). What is your objective, and why is it important to you?

2. Specify the behavioral steps or activities you will do in the room to begin the activity and behave per your aims.

3. How do you become "off track"? What may jeopardise your plans? Predict a potential obstacle or distraction you may face while working on the activity.

4. How will you deal with the disruption? Create an "IF-THEN" method for coping with this barrier/distraction. ("IF I come across X, THEN I shall deal with it by performing Y").

5. Follow your step-by-step strategy and "enter the room with a plan" to carry out your desired activity.

ESTABLISH BEGINNING AND END OF TASKS

Many chores and meetings – such as college courses, job meetings, religious events, television shows, a time-based exercise regimen, and so on –

have defined (or at least relatively predictable) start and finish times. Because they are time-bound, these tasks are easy to organize and fit around other obligations in your daily planner.

Many projects do not have such strict time constraints. You may want to perform some housekeeping or write on a paper for a course, but no one will know if you do not complete these duties. It is simple to justify, "I can work on this later."

If you work on it later, it won't be an issue. However, time constraints are a serious issue for individuals with ADHD and anxiety. Many people report putting off work or a task (such as having clean clothes or cleaning up their space) until the last minute.

Tasks with no clear ends are more difficult to plan. You've seen road signs near major cities informing drivers about the expected journey time to different exits and interchanges. Even though there would be a delay, drivers may modify their attitudes and expectations when given a firm time estimate to their destination instead of it being ambiguous. It is the same with tasks placed into the daily planner—it is useful to know when they begin and when they will conclude to modify expectations and encourage follow-through.

Many individuals with ADHD and anxiety claim that they "work best at the last minute," yet those who seek therapy for ADHD frequently experience severe issues (Hallowell, 2022) of this habit of "brinkmanship." Even if you can pull an "all-nighter" or spend long sessions catching up on work or housework (both of which are romanticized as "hyperfocus"), these tactics come at a cost to your physical and mental well-being. Setting end deadlines for projects mitigate the chance of getting into this crisis cycle.

A coping method for open-ended work that uses the daily planner style is to plan realistic start and finish times. Projects like writing a research paper for college, preparing a presentation for work, or cleaning and arranging a space at home may be overwhelming. People may spend many hours on any of these vital chores without accomplishment.

Although these are the chores for which you should set aside time in your daily planner, there will almost certainly never be enough time to perform them all at once. Even if you have a free calendar with no obligations, it is unlikely that you or anybody else would arrange and complete an eight-hour block of time dedicated to "cleaning and organising my bedroom" or "writing the prescribed 20-page paper." You don't spend that much time on things you like, much alone a task or project.

First and foremost, you should intend for the start and finish dates to be reasonable and attainable expectations for work performance, especially those that are not inherently fun or "motivating." Using the previous example, you may not be able to commit to cleaning a room for eight hours, but you will be able to manage 30 minutes. You're still doing a job, but you're reducing your attention and expectations by setting a time limit for a task that is reasonable and allows you to participate in a constructive activity. This coping approach is another step in "breaking down chores" to make them more manageable. Rather than increasing your desire for the activity, try "lowering the bar" and setting a more fair expectation.

A second advantage of having start and finish times is that it makes work scheduling easy, fostering follow-through. These are the chores you should usually put on your daily to-do list. This method is handy when working on a huge project that cannot be finished all at once. You choose a certain section of the project to focus on within a set period, allowing you to make progress without feeling overwhelmed (and then procrastinating).

Finally, using start and finish times for assignments is a good method to manage days when you have a lot of free time, such as a leisure day or a weekend. This free time does not mean that you have to be "productive" all day and plan everything. However, this strategy may assist in identifying certain appropriate duties (including entertainment and downtime) that can serve as anchors throughout the day and prevent the sensation of coming to the conclusion of a "free day" and feeling like it was a waste.

ACTIVITIES FOR SELF-CARE

It is critical to prioritize self-care, including your health and wellness, via activities such as exercise, meditation, hobbies, and relaxation. You may believe that these are "simple" things that take up too much of your time and that you should be focusing on more productive duties.

Yes, you are more prone to put off necessary tasks that are not instantly reinforcing. ADHD, on the other hand, hinders planning as well as following through on personal interests. We do not want you to abandon fun hobbies, but rather be more conscious of how they fit into your day and be proactive in scheduling time for them as a reward for the time spent on other duties. Balancing your energy and effort is part of the rhythm of your timetable.

It is critical to arrange breaks during the day, providing time for meals and exercise, among other things. Because of the attention and poor self-monitoring characteristics of ADHD and anxiety, you may miss indications that you are hungry, tired, or other signs about your present physical condition that influence your performance. Making time for self-care ensures that you pay attention to your well-being.

One impediment to prioritizing self-care is the idea, "I can't think about exercise when I have so much to accomplish" (or "I wasted my time earlier in the day; therefore, I can't justify allowing myself to continue the exercise." We see self-care (and recreational) duties as critical to encouraging the completion of other "work" and "education" tasks, as well as any other significant commitments.

Self-care is crucial to enhancing general well-being and productivity, rather than "wasting time." Of course, there may be occasions when you must sacrifice a self-care action for another goal (for example, "I will have to forego my downtime on the Internet today to be ready for my speech tomorrow."). However, it is generally good to continue self-care activities and not deprive oneself of the benefits that sleep, exercise, and a balanced diet give.

Statements of logic:

• "I'm not going to sit here and let my anxiousness fester." "I'm going to get up and walk around to get rid of this extra adrenaline."

• "I don't have to deal with this right now. Instead, I'm going to burn it off deliberately."

• "I'm committed to keep going ahead and permanently reducing this anxiety!"

When in doubt, take action. Move around and get some exercise. While this is not a long-term solution to this situation, it is something you can do every day to improve your mood and keep you physically fit. Excessive worrying, as well as anticipatory anxiety, are reduced by exercise. Anything that might briefly alleviate our anxiousness is beneficial and is a step in the right direction.

So, remember not to sit motionlessly, dwell, or be afraid. Don't succumb to defeat. Instead, get up, leave, and get going. By getting more active, you may reduce your anticipatory worry.

THE IMPORTANCE OF MEDICATION

Many adults with ADHD need medication as part of their therapy. Medicine does not treat ADHD; instead, it alleviates symptoms while active.

Certain neurotransmitters appear to be predominantly and directly affected by medications that most successfully address the primary symptoms of ADHD. The neurotransmitters responsible for this are dopamine and norepinephrine. Both neurotransmitters seem to be involved in ADHD's attentional and behavioral symptoms. A pharmaceutical trial may assist in establishing which treatment works best for each person and at what dose. Typically, the study starts with a low dosage progressively raised at three to seven-day stages until clinical advantages are obtained.

Medication usage reports differ. For some, the benefits are enormous; for others, medicine is beneficial; and for others, the outcomes are small. Attention span, impulsivity, and on-task behavior frequently improve in organized situations. Some adolescents increase their frustration tolerance, cooperation, and even their penmanship. Interactions with families, friends, and educators may improve as well.

CHAPTER 5
TIME AND TASK MANAGEMENT
DEFINE, PRIORITIZE, AND CONSTRUCT WHAT YOU DO

Y ou have the essential tools to manage your time, projects, effort, and energy if you have a notion of your complete to-do list, prioritising a daily to-do list, and a daily planner system. You may have created numerous intricate lists and well-designed strategies in the past but did not follow through on them. Thus, how successfully you control your ADHD and anxiety is determined by how well you play the time management game.

This chapter will concentrate on time management "moves" and techniques that will assist you in putting together the many skills and tools we've examined so far to follow through on plans.

TASKS CAN BE DEFINED IN SPECIFIC AND BEHAVIORAL TERMS, AND THIS IS HOW TO DO IT

What is the specific task you are avoiding? What are your first instincts in response to this task? Is there any way to characterise the assignment to encourage completion?

We've spoken about the need to describe a job or activity in as clear and behavioral terms as feasible. On your to-do list or in your daily planner, you may have items such as "work on the yearly update," "clean up the house," "exercise," or "do readings for economics class."

Some people may interpret these brief statements into action plans, such as utilising the plan to "clean up the kitchen" as a trigger to empty the dishwasher. Individuals with ADHD, and anxiety, on the other hand, have difficulty converting these broadly defined activities into a particular sequence of behaviors that encourages follow-through ("There is too much to accomplish. I'm at a loss for words. This is too much for me right now.").

It is helpful to express your goal in particular behavioral phrases or action steps that you may do on your daily to-do list or while carrying out such chores. For more significant projects comprising several more minor activities, such as a monthly report or cleaning up a room, defining a minor component step offers you an attainable aim that keeps you motivated.

To put it another way, you want to "lower the bar" to enhance the chance of getting started.

Working on the yearly report, for instance, might be redefined as "spend 30 minutes analysing the sales figures for the last year" or "use last year's report as a framework to input information for this year." "Cleaning up the house" may mean "removing rugs and furniture to clean." This approach is a variation in breaking down a major work into smaller pieces. Of course, we've all heard this advice and know what we should do, but the key here is to plan out how we'll accomplish it, down to the tiniest initial step that bridges the gap between inactivity and action (Hofmann, 2007).

In contrast, persistent procrastination on a task might indicate that you do not yet have a clear beginning point. The next part focuses on approaches to describe the critical initial step that distinguishes between procrastination and involvement.

ESTABLISH THE MOST IMPORTANT TASKS FOR YOUR TO-DO LIST

After determining your primary commitments and duties for the day; it is critical to align your calendar with your daily to-do list. Activities on your daily to-do list, such as completing a particular errand or committing time to an essential work or school assignment, may be planned in your daily planner.

For instance, you may have a weekly 2 p.m. class noted as an obligation in your daily planner, but you do not need to include it on your daily to-do list. If you are due to give a presentation at the next class meeting, you may designate the break before that session in your planner for final touches, which is an item on the daily to-do list.

The daily planner is similar to Google Maps in that you may begin with a broad view of the overall region and the path you will follow. You may zoom in on increasingly more comprehensive views of particular weeks, days, and segments of a single day, similar to the map function. The daily to-do list becomes the street-level view, in which you get to a task using step-by-step guidance. Of course, as with excellent instructions, having appropriate and correct steps for these activities (Hallowell, 2022), which we will describe next, is essential.

BEHAVIORAL ENGAGEMENT - START BY DEFINING THE SMALLEST STEPS

Despite the above-listed solutions, you may still have trouble getting started on activities. The types of work on which you continue to procrastinate are probably those for which even modest steps are relatively tedious or uncomfortable, such as chores, academic duties (reading textbooks, writing assignments), or administrative responsibilities of adult life (dealing with taxes or finances).

These and other chores elicit unpleasant ideas and sentiments which impede follow-through, even on the first steps. To get started on these activities, describe the simplest actions necessary to begin the activity in rigorous, behavioral phases. These early actions may not include finishing the work, but they are important stages (Hofmann, 2007) that allow you to "touch" a task rather than keep it at arm's length.

This method is intended to assist you in breaking down jobs into their specific behavioral components, similar to a food recipe. "I don't know how to cook," you may remark, or "I can't do it." However, after you follow the listed procedures, you are involved in the job rather than separated from it. It's a beneficial task to see how other activities are broken down into steps. Do it by yourself.

A college attendee, for instance, may have academic tasks for many courses. She schedules 30 minutes for one of the readings, intending to go as far as she can in that time. Despite knowing that it is necessary, she cannot tear himself away from the computer to begin the reading. The initial stage in behavioral engagement is to cease the task interfering with the goal and then take the smallest possible step toward the target task.

For the college student, the objective becomes "get up and go pick up the textbook." The following step is to "open to the first page of the chapter." The next stage is to "read the opening line of the chapter," which the student is now doing. Now, she is no longer delaying the task. She may quit reading after the first phrase or after 12 minutes, or she can read for the whole 30 minutes (and beyond). Whatever occurs next, the student now has an action-based framework for dealing with procrastination rather than merely attempting to "not procrastinate."

"This is so simple, it won't assist me," you may think in response to this coping tip. However, if you are delaying duties, it is clear that something is wrong with your attitude. As an illustration, it may seem silly to have to manage a phone call by defining the first step as "pick up a receiver" or "find the individual in my contact list." Still, most individuals with ADHD have instances of task procrastination that are equally absurd ("I can't believe I still haven't made that phone call. I could have blown my chance."). The first stage of behavioral engagement is to define a job as such an embarrassingly easy action step that failing to complete it becomes silly (Hofmann, 2007).

We invite you to do an experiment where you just observe how you postpone chores throughout your day to discover how you do not complete things. Of course, not all work delays result from procrastination, but the experiment illustrates the process.

It may be anything as basic as not cleaning up a crumpled piece of paper on the floor that had bounced off the edge of a trash can, or it could be something more personal, such as a job assignment or an exercise. The practice requires you to assist yourself in observing the many thoughts, emotions, and escape actions that comprise your procrastination profile. Procrastination is a habit that may become automatic, like tying your shoes.

The capacity to notice the indicators of procrastination as they emerge, on the other hand, helps to make the process less automatic, offers signals that you are postponing work, and opens up multiple intervention opportunities for using your coping methods.

The tactics listed above intend for you to get you to the brink of your preferred action plan. Finally, you must take that first step that signifies truly accomplishing what you set out to achieve. Each of the above phases will assist you in preparing for the work and taking figurative baby steps toward completion rather than instantly sliding into the over-learned habit of procrastination.

It's crucial to realise that you may not be "in the mood" to complete the activity or action. In reality, keep in mind that you may overestimate how little energy and attention are necessary to begin work. The last push to begin a task or activity is analogous to legislative "swing votes"—it does not have to be unanimous; merely reaching a 51–49 outcome is sufficient to initiate behavioral involvement. "Once I got started," most people say, "it wasn't as horrible as I feared."

BREAKING A TASK OR ACTIVITY INTO STEPS

Zeno's paradoxes is a philosophical puzzle collection. While attempting to leave a place, you must first reach the halfway point between yourself and the exit. As you go toward the doorway, you will reach a new midway, and each subsequent attempt to depart the area will need you to reach the next midpoint.

The paradox is that you should be unwilling to leave a room since you can endlessly reduce the distance to the exit without ever leaving. When confronted with chores on your daily to-do list, you may often feel like you are attempting to leave the room since it seems as if you can never get things started.

Zeno's paradox demonstrates how most jobs are broken down into ever-smaller component pieces. More significantly, taking the appropriate initial step toward completing a job provides you the confidence that "I can do this."

When laying out your priority duties, you will come across certain jobs that cause you to feel fear, overwhelmed, or as if you can't cope with them. Rather than reflexively ignoring them ("I can't manage this right now!"), the first step is to assess what you want to achieve and if your objective – at least as you presently see it – is too large or imprecise. The general goal remains vital, such as "arrange my room" or "work on paper for school," but it is difficult to see a means to get started in such broad terms.

You may break the major project into its component phases like you would leave a room. Thus, "arrange my room" is divided into three tasks: eliminating clutter that does not belong in the space, selecting what objects will remain in the room, and determining where each kept item belongs.

Even the initial step of decluttering may be too stressful. If such is the case, you can reduce this step to a single item, such as "I will begin by picking up any dishes in my room and taking them to the kitchen." Similarly, a job or school project is divided into phases. Before diving into the monthly report write-up, data may need to be gathered or examined (Hofmann, 2007).

Time spent organising one's ideas or preparing a paper might assist a student to start a project without needing to leap immediately into writing. Even if you have begun your write-up, you may put off returning to the incomplete document. The aim of "continue writing the report" is demanding; therefore, word the first, smaller step toward this goal as "I will read the previous paragraph I wrote and then write the first line of the following paragraph."

The key concepts describe the task in basic and behavioral terms to transform the task goal into an activity you can do. To combat procrastination, you will be able to reduce most projects to the simplest initial step that you feel capable of doing.

A simple method to begin "touching" work and school assignments are to ensure you have accurate information about the task's limits, due date, and so on (e.g., "I will review the syllabus to ensure I am clear about the assignment."). Simply opening a computer file for a work assignment or picking up a textbook to study for a class are basic action steps that dramatically boost the chance of completing the activity.

Time spent imagining and preparing the activity is a little step of involvement and an exposure exercise that improves your capacity to confront something you normally avoid and flee. A spreadsheet, a piece of paper, or index cards may be used to separate the many parts of a huge project, including your starting point, the targeted end point, and all the intermediate phases. This practice is beneficial when a job is vast and has a deadline.

This kind of undertaking necessitates "doing a little bit" each day instead of completing everything at the last minute in a frenzy. Even if you intend to commit an hour or two to an activity, such as housework, errands, or yard maintenance, a strategy for breaking down and arranging your actions is beneficial (which can include a reward). Breaking an activity down into manageable steps is an important method for getting started and staying on track.

REALISTIC EXPECTATIONS - THIS IS HOW TO ESTABLISH THEM

The film Apollo 13 dramatized a human space trip to the Moon in 1970. Due to technical problems, the space trip was aborted mid-flight. The mission's goal shifted from landing on the Moon to returning the men to Earth successfully. The astronauts' damaged spaceship had an insufficient battery capacity to power the various computer systems required to reenter Earth's atmosphere. NASA experts on the ground had to figure out the best way to reactivate these systems while conserving energy and without emptying the batteries (Hallowell, 2022).

Some individuals with ADHD and anxiety prioritize morning exercise (Hofmann, 2007), which allows them to concentrate on high-priority chores first thing in the morning before moving on to other things. Others like to "warm up" with lower-priority administrative activities first thing in the morning before tackling higher-priority, more difficult tasks.

Students learn that some times of the day are preferable to others for focusing on academic duties, such as dedicating mornings to writing projects and afternoons to required readings. Similarly, specific pivot points in the day might be recognized as excellent times for monotonous chores, such as sorting through the mail as soon as you get home from work or trying to catch up on emails for 15 minutes after coming from a lunch break at work.

Understanding "how your brain works" is critical to planning your timetable and honestly judging how well your routine works. Someone else's adaptive warm-up task is another person's escape behavior. The trick is to figure out what is feasible and sustainable for you.

DO NOT BE AFRAID TO MAKE NECESSARY CHANGES

Life is unpredictable. Situations may develop that will need adjusting your expectations and plans, such as skipping work to pick up a sick kid from school or attending an emergency automobile repair. Aside from the technicalities of restructuring your calendar, the daily planner also serves as a coping aid for managing, or at the very least reducing, the emotional stress that comes with unanticipated changes.

Using your planner allows you to see what adjustments you need to make and how to accomplish them. To accomplish a job by a deadline, you may have to compromise, such as missing a gym visit or delaying an appointment. Having a record of your planned obligations, on the other hand, gives a framework for dealing with the issue by taking the required measures to cancel and reschedule appointments, as well as any other modifications that must be made to successfully "handle the problem."

In addition to dealing with an unexpected change in your schedule, the daily planner assists you in determining if the occurrence was unexpected or whether it was the consequence of procrastinating or underestimating the importance of particular chores. These abilities and processes enable you to learn from errors more orderly and reduce their recurrence.

PLANS FOR IMPLEMENTATION

The reality of coping with procrastination is that you will face many distractions and lower-priority chores that are simpler, more pleasurable, or just emerge as handy reasons for flight after your early zeal wears off. It is beneficial to have implementation strategies in place to ensure follow-through.

Implementation intention plans, based on research on children with ADHD, are intended to externalise executive functioning by predicting challenges to your aims and preparing strategies to manage those threats.

Consider these tactics to be malware for threats to your time management strategy.

A college student, for example, who expects to study an assigned material for 30 minutes would almost certainly confront several distractions. Even if he's reading at the library, he could see a buddy pass by, get a text message, or have a spontaneous idea about something he wants to do later. Each of these harmless diversions has the potential to throw him off course.

Develop detailed plans for these occurrences as part of the implementation plans. Using if-then plans to build a strategy for starting, such as "If I go to the library, then I will read for at least 30 minutes," or "If I encounter a friend, then I will tell her I have to finish reading but will see her later" are excellent ways to start these detailed plans.

Instead of continuously concentrating on an overarching goal to sustain motivation, implementation plans address particular threats to the current plan (which is part of a bigger aim), compatible with the approach of "entering the room with a plan." Given how readily people with ADHD may be diverted, we focused on establishing these if-then strategies to deal with different task-interfering distractions, transitions between activities, returning after breaks, etc.

There's no assurance you won't get sidetracked or succumb to distraction. Being interested in the activity, thinking through possible distractions, and building your adaptive reactions (including preemptive steps like turning off your phone) all work together to raise the possibility of greater follow-through on your objectives than in the past. Furthermore, these approaches give you steps to engage or reconnect with tasks (Hofmann, 2007).

ESCAPE THAT HABITS INTRODUCTION

Regardless of the coping mechanisms discussed above, including implementation tactics, it is important to know the distractions you are subject to while procrastinating. You will develop a list of "usual suspects" of escape behaviors, which may include checking your email, social media usage, or other things that, if not pleasurable, are less stressful than the possibility of your job plans.

It is important to transition from not realizing they procrastinated to acknowledging that they were engaging in escape behavior. These "escape" activities may be exploited as task completion incentives, shifting their behavioral function from negative reinforcement of off-task behavior to positive reinforcement of on-task conduct.

What are the most typical jobs, websites, devices, games, etc.? If you find yourself doing them, are you avoiding something else? Instead of completing a key job, such as cleaning or napping, are there other useful activities you can do instead of completing a key job?

Procrastination is a combination of actions that result in the postpone-ment of duties. To begin rewriting your procrastination "script," you must first comprehend it and unravel the different aspects that put you at risk for this behavior. Another important aspect of combating procrastination is controlling your thoughts about what you set out to do.

PROCRASTINATION AND ITS RELATED THOUGHTS

Your current attitude toward a task is an important component of the procrastination script. We're talking about the reflexive or instinctive thoughts and emotions you have when faced with a priority task (or any other kind of activity you wish to perform). Each job on your daily to-do list was specified in behavioral terms, sounded attainable, and was a priority when you created it. You were probably more excited about the potential of taking action and your capacity to do so.

However, when confronted with the work, you discover that your perspective has shifted. You begin to believe that you are not up to this right now and that there are so many other annoying jobs you can get done right now; it would be better for you to accomplish them instead of this other duty.

You are suddenly off doing something else, possibly even realising that you are delaying. Later, when you discover you did not stick to your plan and wasted crucial time, you feel bad about yourself, thinking, "I had plenty of time to do this today. Again, how did I do this? I'm not sure when I'll have the opportunity to focus on it in the next few days, and I'm racing the clock. This is terrible!"

The description above is not comments made by you or others but rather descriptions of your current flow of ideas or self-talk. These "automatic ideas" regarding your top priorities happen without your conscious knowledge. You may be unaware of how swiftly and powerfully they impact your emotions and behavior. The concepts felt realistic while bouncing around in your mind but ultimately counterproductive.

Cognitive behavioral therapy's "cognitive" component is how this automatic thinking is managed. Negative or distorted thinking does not correlate with ADHD, but as the case above shows, it does not make living with ADHD any easier. When people without ADHD postpone a task, they experience similar ideas, but they can modify their behaviors to guarantee timely follow-through.

Adults with ADHD, on the other hand, constantly relapse into the same procrastination cycle despite suffering consequences. Capturing and modifying these habitual thoughts is a vital coping skill to master.

The first step in addressing negative automatic thoughts regarding work or goal is to catch them by asking, "What am I thinking right now?" These ideas are sometimes stated in quick phrases rather than grammatically perfect sentences ("Oh no," "I loathe this stuff," a series of expletives, etc.). In truth, procrastination may begin with a true statement ("The gym is packed after work.") However, this might set off a chain of assumptions that lead to procrastination ("I won't be able to locate any available equipment, so I won't be able to complete my exercise. I'm too tired to deal with crowds, so I won't go tonight."). That evening watching TV and eating too many cheese puffs led to self-criticism and irritation with the missed exercise ("I could have gone to the gym. I would have finished by now. Now I have to find time to make up for the lost time.").

It is critical to be conscious of how your ideas cause you to postpone. Automatic thoughts are frequently distorted and influence your sentiments about work. You begin to freak yourself out of completing anything without having a chance to start, increasing the possibility of turning to avoid work via an escape habit.

You must:

1. Determine the specific task that you are putting off.

2. Identify your ideas about completing the work. How do you exaggerate the bad parts of a task?

3. Identify your thoughts regarding the activity, such as boredom or a gut sensation of "ugh, I don't want to do this."

4. Now, consider and emphasise why this work is important to you and how it will feel to do it.

5. Identify the favourable characteristics of your capacity to do the work that you may lessen.

6. Consider how happy you will feel after you have completed the assignment.

7. If Regardless of how you feel, break down the work into tiny, initial steps you can do to get started.

8. Allow yourself a few seconds of pain and doubt while taking step #7.

9. You have stopped procrastinating.

CHAPTER 6
MOTIVATION, EMOTIONS, AND ENERGY

The vast majority of obligations you will encounter in life will necessitate consistent and numerous efforts over time to accomplish or sustain, such as finishing a large project for work, keeping up with school tasks, performing home repairs, or recurring tasks, such as paying bills, preserving an exercise routine, trying to manage household chores, and so on.

"Sometimes I can get started on a goal and stay going for a short while, but I cannot sustain it," many people with ADHD and anxiety remark (Hallowell, 2022), which is a characteristic of the executive dysfunction and motivational deficiencies that underpin ADHD.

While different planning, organisational skills, and other "getting started" skills will continue to be helpful, there are extra measures you can take to keep your plan on track, remain on top of things, and avoid spiraling into chronic and painful procrastination.

MOTIVATION - PRODUCE IT!

When dealing with the subject of plan follow-through, the question of motivation often comes up. Many individuals with ADHD and anxiety may strive to attain a goal (exercise) or complete a certain task (test, paying bills) but, despite their best efforts, succumb to an apparent lack of drive. This circumstance reminds us of a comment attributed to the late fitness instructor Jack LaLanne, stating at the age of 93, "I'm feeling terrific, and I still have sex nearly every day." Returning to the executive dysfunction perspective of ADHD, motivation is described as the capacity to develop a feeling about a task that supports follow-through without immediate reward or consequence (and often in the face of some short-term pain).

In other words, motivation is the capacity to make oneself "feel like" executing a job even when there is no compelling reason to do so. Consequently, you'll have to find a method to make yourself want to exercise or prepare for a midterm test that's still a few days away before you get the results you want.

You "know" cognitively that these are wonderful ideas, but bad sentiments (including boredom) or a lack of enthusiasm about a task undermine your efforts to begin. One of the most prevalent cognitive mistakes shown by individuals with ADHD while delaying is the exaggeration of emotional unpleasantness connected with commencing a task, generally accompanied by a reduction in the good sensations associated with it.

Adults with ADHD face the double disadvantage of having more trouble creating positive feelings (motivation) required to participate in activities and having more difficulty resisting the temptation of more immediate distractions, particularly those that give an escape from pain. Individuals with ADHD have frequently had more than their fair share of difficulties and failures in many critical facets of their life from a developmental viewpoint.

In our view, many daily tasks and activities have been connected with a degree of stress and little apparent reward, exacerbating the motivational issues that ADHD individuals already confront.

We will use the metaphor of food poisoning to demonstrate how one's learning history because of ADHD poses (Hallowell, 2022) impedes pursuing important personal objectives. Food poisoning is caused by consuming contaminated food. It is an adaptive reaction in which your brain and digestive system detect the presence of a toxin in your body and respond with nausea and quick evacuation of the toxin by diarrhea, vomiting, or both.

Even after you have completely recovered and determined that you had food poisoning, the sight and smell of the meal, even before it reaches your lips, can revive protective emotions of nausea owing to the past connection of the stimulus (the food) with disease and discomfort. You may make all the rational reasons for your safety and assurances that the meal is safe, but your body will still have this first unpleasant response. To break the food poisoning connection, increasing exposure to unspoiled morsels of the meal is required (often mixing it in with "safe" food in difficult situations).

Similarly, in your attempts to build and maintain excellent habits for controlling ADHD, you will come into certain chores that cause pain while recognizing the importance of the work at hand. As a result, it is critical to generate just enough drive to shift out of avoidance and take a "taste" of the work you are putting off.

You will need to feel like performing the activity you are avoiding, at least enough to take the initial steps toward doing it. Performing the activity does not imply that you must be zealous about what you want to under-take. You simply need to know that you can carry out your immediate action plan, even if you are not "in the mood" to do so.

This kind of motivation is developed by narrowing your attention to the processes required to engage in the desired goal. Starting a task frequently alters your perspective because you deal with the reality of your actions rather than being lost in anticipations and ambivalence.

Furthermore, once you take the initial step toward completing the assign-ment, you are no longer delayed. Rather than striving to increase your motivation to meet the demands of the activity, you may decrease (Hofmann, 2007) the initial demands of the task to match your existing motivation level and get to the point where you declare, "I can do this."

As described in the preceding chapter, taking little actions to "touch" a task allows you to get started on it without needing to feel motivated—action frequently precedes motivation. Returning to the food poisoning metaphor, these procedures assist you in tasting a little enough piece of the previously hazardous food to enable you to rebuild good associations with it and allow your brain and body to feel secure again. In implementing strategies to manage ADHD better, you may encounter some deeply ingrained avoidance habits that seem immune to change and take more specific effort to overcome.

ENERGY - MANAGE IT!

Time management entails energy management as well. The explanation for procrastinating is often wrapped up in the remark "I'm not up to this," which reflects the reality that you are fatigued, stressed, or in some other unpleasant condition. You infer that you lack the necessary energy to complete a work, which is likely accompanied by a mistaken explanation for postponing it ("I have to be at my best or else I will be unable to accomplish it.").

Comparable to reframing time, reframing energy might help you respond to the "I'm not up to this" emotion. Thinking through a work's actual behavioral and energy needs provides a more accurate perspective on the original and sometimes skewed rationale. Remember that you simply need "enough" energy to get started. As a result, being "too weary" to empty the dishwasher or do the laundry might be reframed to perceive these duties as taking just a little energy and concentration.

Utilising this kind of reframing to address automatic ideas regarding energy on activities that demand a bit extra pep in the step. For example, it is typical for individuals to be hesitant to exercise because they believe they are "too fatigued to exercise." That assumption may be shifted to reflect the energy necessary for the minor stages in the "exercise script" that serve as the "launch sequence" for going to the gym ("Are you too tired to retrieve your workout clothes? Carry them to the car?" and so on). You may also ask yourself whether you've ever seen somebody slumped over the workout equipment at the gym because they ran out of energy from attempting to push themselves when they were "too weary."

Instead, you may rely on prior experience to know that you will feel better and more invigorated after exercising; you will sleep much better, be more rested, and benefit from sticking to your exercise schedule. At the very least, going through this process rather than succumbing to the want to avoid increases (Hofmann, 2007) the likelihood that you will make a reasoned choice rather than an impulsive one regarding the assignment.

A specific energy management problem essential to sticking to plans is your capacity to sustain energy (and hence effort) over extended periods. Anxiety management is an endurance sport. Good soccer players are known to find their rest on the field to play the whole 90 minutes of a game. Likewise, you must control your speed and effort throughout the day. The rhythm of your daily planner's many chores and duties influences your energy. It is critical to participate in self-care throughout the day, including proper sleep, mealtime, rest, and recreational activities to recharge your batteries.

Even at work, you may follow up a demanding activity – such as working on a project – with more administrative activities – such as replying to emails or phone conversations – that do not take as much mental energy or, at the very least, indicate a transition to a new task. Similarly, you may complete different duties earlier in the evening and spend the remainder of the time resting at home.

A good reminder is that there are methods to make certain jobs manageable, if not joyful, by tying them to favored hobbies for which you have greater drive. Folding clothes while watching the television or performing yard work or domestic duties while listening to music on an iPod, are instances of how you can combine responsibilities and pleasure hobbies. Furthermore, enjoyable experiences and job accomplishments will most likely be satisfying and stimulating.

THE BENEFITS OF REWARD SYSTEMS

The usage of reward systems is another fundamental behavioral concept that can improve motivation and follow-through. The Premack Principle is a well-established psychological concept that states that following the accomplishment of a less wanted job with the reward of an extremely desirable task increases the chance of doing the less desired task. Examples of the idea include eating veggies before dessert and completing schoolwork before watching television.

A pleasant reward acts as a carrot at the end of a stick to incentivize a work that is not intrinsically joyful. The reward should be something you want and, preferably, something you can only have by finishing that activity. For example, you may reward regular exercise with a fruit smoothie or completion of a study session for a final test with a music download.

These behavioral goals are not immutable physical rules. You will be tempted to break them ("I want a smoothie but don't feel like moderate exercise will be an advantage on tomorrow's exercise."). The mere linkage of activity with a reward, on the other hand, will most certainly boost its salience for you. At the very least, it causes a halt in time and action (behavioral suppression) that enables you to think about the job rather than putting it off impulsively.

HOW TO ACCEPT AND RETRAIN YOUR EMOTIONS

Another aspect of living with ADHD that you should be aware of is that you will most likely have difficulty managing your emotions. This diffi-culty may not always imply that you suffer from a mood or anxiety issue. Rather, emotional regulation challenges associated with ADHD are char-acterized by difficulty with emotions in circumstances that most individuals experience, whether unfavourable, such as dealing with job stress, or positive, such as receiving exciting news.

While anybody will have an emotional response to upsetting news – such as a large car repair costs or an unforeseen and inconvenient change in one's work schedule – the individual with ADHD is more likely to overreact, which may cause additional stress. Someone with ADHD may take longer to cool down, later realising their anger was unwarranted but then having to cope with the consequences of the response in addition to the initial cause of stress.

Thus, controlling ADHD necessitates the development of "emotional endurance" for dealing with things that, in the short term, you do not want to accomplish but that, in the long run, are associated with cherished objectives. Again, executive dysfunction makes these undertakings more challenging for those with ADHD. When confronted with duties or events that cause emotional distress, it is critical to realise that the only way out is to follow the event through to the end.

You will often suffer pain when confronted with chores that you normally avoid. A coping skill in these instances is the knowledge that you can identify your emotions, describe them, and yet follow through on the actions needed in the work you want to do, even if you are still uncomfortable.

Our elementary approach to mindful tolerance of emotional pain associated with ADHD management is the capacity to detect emotions, tolerate them, and remain on track with what you are doing. Just as you may have to accomplish something despite a headache, there will be certain things that you can do despite an emotional "pain," which is frequently worrying, boredom, or a sense of "ugh."

One emotional management tactic is to behave in the opposite direction of your present mood, known as the "method acting" approach or behaving "as if." If you are furious about anything, you may make yourself grin or clap your hands together and say loudly, "okay, enough TV, it is time to tackle my report" to get started on a job.

Merging these skills with other task engagement methods – like defining the first step and setting reasonable time expectations – helps you respond to the task and changes your relationship with these emotions to tolerate them rather than eliminating them as a precondition to starting the task.

As you begin to face tasks that you have previously avoided, you will discover that you are better able to do so without being distracted by your emotions. You will still have sentiments about specific chores, but they will be less likely to throw you off course, offering new and lucrative opportunities for you.

You must:

1. Recognize your emotional responses that lead to your avoidance of an urgent duty.

2. Recognize your sensations, such as boredom, slight anticipation, or "Ugh" ("I don't want to do this right now.")

3. Place your "discomfort" on a scale. How powerful is it? Rate it on a scale of 0 (relaxed) to 10 (worst agony I've ever felt).

4. Notice your feeling and how it feels without attempting to suppress it.

5. Concentrate on breathing slowly and steadily through your emotions.

6. Recognize that your emotions do not have to control your actions.

7. Consider that you can carry out your ambitions while feeling some difficulty.

8. Participate in and concentrate on the lowest behavioral stage for your job.

9. Pay attention to what happens to your emotions after you begin working on the activity.

10. Put these abilities to use in different situations and jobs throughout the day.

EMOTIONAL MANAGEMENT IN INTERACTIONS

In addition to empathy abilities, having a game plan for dealing with emotions generated in these situations is beneficial. There are things you can "do" in these circumstances to effectively manage them, similar to our advice to "make chores manual" to encourage follow through. To begin, determine your "role" or task in the circumstance.

For instance, your position may be "I am an employee listening to what my employer has to say" or "I will be a spouse listening to my wife's views." Classifying your role in an encounter aids in the development of a behavioral script that you may follow, including how you manage your emotions.

Whatever position you play in a circumstance, exposure to distressing information is always a threat. As a result, the second step is to remind oneself to be a good listener and refrain from interrupting the speaker.

It is often beneficial to concentrate on your breathing and keep your muscles relaxed, such as by letting your arms drop freely at your sides. Throughout the encounter, employ empathetic actions and remarks to assist you in concentrating on the task at hand.

Lastly, you will need some time away from the scene following the contact to reflect on what you heard. Even when confronted with a difficult circumstance, things frequently look much more rational and controllable after a few minutes of absorbing them (however, ADHD-related emotion regulation may undermine this viewpoint). You may then return to your "role" description to decide on your plan of action based on the input (for example, "My employer expects me to be on time or I will be written up. Allow me to devise a fresh strategy for getting to work on time.").

Furthermore, after the first wave of emotion has passed, you will most likely have a better perspective on the topic and will be able to detect favourable input you may have gotten but ignored.

The way you approach an encounter has a significant impact on the result. Being able to hear someone out demonstrates your dedication to them. The purpose of developing empathy skills is to remain involved in a dialogue in a productive, in-the-moment way and accept and manage critique. Informing someone that they're correct makes their fury tough to increase.

Because dealing with criticism from others may be a sensitive place for individuals with ADHD, we have presented several communication and empathy techniques. However, you may use the same coping skills to provide feedback to others, bring up sensitive problems, or ask for assistance. For example, if your husband often changes the basket at the front entrance that you use to keep a record of your keys and cell phone so you don't miss them, you will feel adaptive and informative anger.

CHAPTER 7
ATTITUDES, BELIEFS, AND SELF ESTEEM
LIVE YOUR BEST LIFE WITH ADHD

Adults with ADHD have frequently suffered more failures and frustrations connected with ADHD symptoms, sometimes without understanding the effect of ADHD on them. When you consider a history of poor grades, forgetting or failing to keep commitments to others, and repetitive exhortations about your untapped potential with the need to work much harder, you may develop a negative self-view.

The long-term effect of these frequent setbacks might be the loss of your sense of self, sometimes known as poor self-esteem. These ingrained, long-lasting self-views, or "basic assumptions" about who you are, are seen as a lens through which you perceive yourself, the world, and your role. Therefore, self-esteem and improving it are the focus of this chapter.

Severe adverse experiences linked with ADHD may unjustly skew your vision, leading to a distorted pessimistic perspective of oneself in specific settings. When confronted with experiences that trigger these negative beliefs in the present, you feel powerful emotions, negative thoughts, and a propensity to engage in self-defeating activities, most often resignation and flight.

These basic beliefs may engage some individuals with ADHD in restricted, particular settings; for others, these beliefs impact one's view in most scenarios. It should be noted that, while feeling perplexed by their symptoms in many locations, many individuals with ADHD have an excellent self-view, even though numerous events temporarily upset their confidence.

CATCHING AND CHANGING YOUR AUTOMATIC THOUGHTS

Our ideas, which include pictures, emotions, norms, and firmly held beliefs, assist us in categorising and making sense of our experiences. We all have a flow of ideas or interpretations of experiences that happen without awareness but can readily recognize when we pay close attention.

Most of these ideas will be neutral and fleeting, with a more excellent positive-to-negative ratio preferred. The essential point is that these reflexive, automatic thoughts are ripe for distortion, which will interfere with your job completion and usage of coping methods.

Automatic thoughts are distorted thoughts, but they are not illusions; rather, they are inaccurate or impulsive judgments about an occurrence in the absence of convincing proof ("I forgot to contact my friend. She must be upset with me."), or that results from a skewed perception ("I got a bad grade on my essay because the teacher dislikes me."). The meaning in each of these situations is reasonable and probable, but the ultimate conclusion cannot be proven, at least not yet.

On the other hand, a distorted thought may trigger subsequent negative thoughts, resulting in a cascade of assumptions, emotions, and actions that launch a self-defeating episode, such as believing that an instructor does not like you, so you will not get a good grade. Because the instructor does not like you, there is no point in attending class.

Because most erroneous ideas negatively tilt events, Cognitive Behavioral Therapy is also referred to as "positive thinking power." However, skewed optimistic beliefs, or what is known as the optimistic illusory bias, may occur in ADHD.

Gambling addicts, for example, are extraordinarily optimistic thinkers, even though their predictions contradict all we know about statistical probability. Recording your spontaneous thoughts is to practice understanding your responses to a situation and how they impact your view, mood, and perceived alternatives for action.

The first step in altering your attitude is just paying attention to your natural thoughts. Being able to stop and examine a situation rather than instinctively responding to it is a basic but crucial ability that indicates a method to practice impulse control.

A simple method to practice detecting these ideas is to pay attention when you have an emotional response to anything in your everyday life, no matter how powerful or mild the reaction, especially when you feel yourself delaying. You may have a visible emotional response to a stressor, but you should note your perception of the scenario and how it may be skewed.

You must:

1. Changes in your sentiments, such as discomfort with a task or the fact that you are avoiding a task, are indicators that you are experiencing negative automatic thoughts.

2. Reflect on the setting, task, or event that generated this emotion.

3. What were your thoughts or interpretations?

4. How does this notion affect your emotions and behavior?

5. Do you make any mistakes in your thinking? What new perspectives may you have?

COMMITMENT AND VALUES

Cognitive techniques, like the tactics for producing motivation outlined above, are vital for maintaining your passion for and dedication to longer-term undertakings. It is too simple to indulge in rationalizations and avoidance tactics to avoid a tough job.

Coping drift may occur after you have made a strong start, such as sifting through your daily mail for many weeks or utilising your daily planner, allowing little deviations from your goals to seep in. What begins as solitary, little deviations from your goals, such as "I'm sleepy now. "I'll take care of this later" leads to you reverting to old behaviors and encountering similar problems, such as paying a late charge for overdue payments.

It is a good exercise to review your reasoning and motives for your coping strategies. If you see your coping patterns slipping, the following questions can assist boost the chance of sticking to a specified plan:

• What aspect of this task do I believe I am incapable of completing?

• Have I ever completed an assignment like this before?

• Do I have to be in a good mood to do this?

• Can I focus on the job for five minutes? What would it be like to achieve progress?

• What pleasant experiences may I have?

• How would it feel to begin this work rather than ignore it?

• How difficult will this assignment truly be? Is it something I can handle?

• Is it okay to do this work only to "cross it off my list"?

In addition to these cognitive tactics for re-establishing commitment, remember what you genuinely value about the activity. The answers to the questions written below might help you nurture and strengthen your dedication to the task:

• What is the significance of this assignment to me?

• How does this activity fit into the bigger picture?

• How far have I progressed toward my final goal? What will be the next step?

• Am I willing to commit to this phase of the plan, even if it is difficult first?

• How will I feel after I finish the task? Will it still seem difficult?

• What are the advantages of beginning this work for me? What are the consequences of procrastination?

• How will it make me feel that I can tackle and complete a challenge like this?

• Can I perform anything relevant to this assignment to know I didn't dodge it?

CHANGE YOUR ATTITUDE

Human negativity bias indicates that humans are programmed to pay greater attention to frightening and terrifying information than good, reassuring information. This bias may be traced back to when early humans sought food, shelter, and water. Humans were always in a fight-or-flight state because of the continual danger of assault, which promotes anxiety.

Anxiety is a physiological reaction when your body creates a lot of adrenaline and enters danger detection mode. While the worry may overestimate danger, the body attempts to keep you safe.

On the other hand, optimism lowers anxiety in individuals with ADHD. Positive thinking, sentiments of hope, goal-directed action, and confidence are all components of optimism. It's not always about seeing the world through rose-colored glasses.

It's all about how you explain what happens to you in your life, particularly the bad stuff, and what you anticipate to happen in the future. This optimism is how you could change your attitude:

1. CHANGE YOUR BRAIN

Our patterns of thinking are neurologically established. It takes time to develop new pathways in our thinking about ourselves, others, and the world.

The brain is very flexible, adaptable, and changing, with the potential to build new connections across sections of the brain that don't interact very well. It takes time, practice, and fresh experiences to help cement new ideas that we are attempting to practice. The orbitofrontal cortex is a portion of the brain critical for incorporating knowledge from the intellectual, logical, and emotional centers and is larger and better developed in individuals who are more optimistic and less worried. You must comprehend that there are several ways of thinking. Then you must think and determine which patterns of thought are troublesome.

For example, by asking a series of questions, you may learn what was going through their minds when the setback occurred and what they thought about it. Then you can figure out how many of your ideas you're utilising to forecast what will occur in the future and what activities you take or don't take.

The most critical factor is to practice new ways of thinking. Many individuals discontinue their efforts before seeing any sustained and occurred change. After doing a lot of thought editing/active therapy, you will spend time modeling the change of mindset and solidifying or storing those thoughts, so they are more accessible to you.

2. BREAK DOWN YOUR FEARS

People with ADHD who are also anxious are likely to have catastrophic thinking, which entails anticipating things to go wrong.They may be tense and find it difficult to relax. They over plan, over worry, and over-think everything. This anxiety is known as a confidence crisis.

Recognizing your fear and learning about it are the antidotes to fear. Understanding the chances of something occurring might help you put your fears into perspective. Many individuals have a mistaken view of the danger that exists in the world. You should remember that 'yes' things may happen, but so can other things. You want to appropriately appraise the possibility of a bad occurrence and your capacity to manage it. Consider a recent distressing occurrence and rate the following on a scale of 0 to 10:

• What are the chances that this will never be resolved or changed?

This book pushes those who tend to exaggerate the chance of something happening to recognize that most situations do resolve themselves over time.

• What are the chances that this occurrence will impact everything in your life?

Considering how the occurrence affects certain areas but not others might help one understand that it isn't as disastrous as first assumed.

• What additional circumstances may have contributed to the occurrence?

It is critical to take ownership of the event's result. Accepting that fear is not the adversary is also a component of this process. There is danger in everything we undertake, and worry exaggerates that risk.

For instance, if you're afraid of making a fool of yourself at school or work, he suggests considering what would happen if that happened and alternative possible outcomes. Is it feasible to speak and have others enjoy what you say? You want to be able to anticipate great possibilities while still understanding that poor results will not kill you.

3. STATE A POSITIVE INTENTION EVERY DAY

Getting out of bed every morning and saying or writing down your objective for the day will help you get into a good frame of mind. Another option to start the day on a good note is to keep a thankful notebook.

When you get up, think about what you value and adjust your mindset from 'I have to' to 'I get to.' For example, instead of expressing, "I have to take my kids to school," try to say, "I have healthy children who are well enough to go to school," or "I have a vehicle to drive my kids to school."

4. SMILE MORE

Sometimes, a smile is the cause of pleasure, and sometimes joy is the cause of a smile. Occasionally we're pleased; therefore, we smile, but sometimes the reverse is true. You may occasionally mislead your body into feeling pleased by smiling.

It is worth noting that biological, mental, and social factors all contribute to anxiety. Mind-body research increasingly demonstrates that thinking stronger affects how the body functions physically.Parts of the brain that govern emotion or may lead to the fight-or-flight reaction, an anxiety reaction that causes strong hormonal effects on the body and impacts several systems, may begin to harm your health.

People who are too worried and under-relaxed, for example, are more likely to get ill. It's why things like exercise and medicine may assist with anxiety and mood regulation, even if they don't directly address what you're thinking — they sort of bypass that and go right to biology. Positive psychology, as well as mindset science, are making strides. Mind-body therapy examines our expectations since what we feel is likely to happen is more likely to occur.

5. BE MINDFUL

Stop and smell the flowers when you're feeling nervous. Being in tune with nature and present through seeing, experiencing, hearing, and inhaling might change your perspective. There is no anxiety if you can be present in the now since anxiety is something that has occurred or will happen.

SIMPLE EXERCISES TO RAISE YOUR SELF ESTEEM

The activities below will assist you in seeing more of the good aspects of yourself and your life. They are designed to immediately increase your self-awareness so that you may enjoy the positive aspects of your life. We have detailed each activity and then discussed why it will help you boost your self-esteem:

• Make a list of ten things you like about yourself.

It is difficult to notice your great qualities when you have a negative attitude. In truth, no one is entirely good or evil. This activity challenges you to search out your good characteristics to enhance your self-image actively. When you're listing them, make a small comment for each one, detailing what you like about it.

Continue if you identify more than ten traits.

When you consider love, you may envision the sort of romantic love seen in Hollywood films. That portrayal of love is not only ridiculous, but it is also not where your ideas of love should begin. Your first love should be yourself since you will not be able to love others until you can love yourself because you can't offer what you don't have.

Self-esteem is a healthy habit of loving yourself. You are a one-of-a-kind and amazing human being with a lot to give the world. You must take the time to recognize this.

The Crucial Point: When I was younger, I was taught that loving oneself was a horrible idea. That is not only false but loving oneself is necessary for a happy and healthy existence. Loving yourself is the easiest and fastest technique to boost your self-esteem.

• List your top ten abilities or skills

Recognising your numerous abilities enables you to recognize how much value and worth you have to give others. Write a short remark for each talent indicating how others could benefit or have benefited from it. Continue if you discover more than ten skills. This basic practice is so effective because it causes you to examine your skill set from a viewpoint you are not presently considering.

When you consider your talents, you are most likely doing so from a position of scarcity. This may be beneficial since it allows you to discover talents that you need to improve. By honing these talents, you may enhance your results in both your professional and personal life. However, if you just evaluate the talents you lack, you will miss out on how immensely skilled you are. You must retain a record of your abilities and characteristics as this guarantees that you have a fair picture of your abilities and will raise your self-esteem.

The Crucial Point: There is no reason for you to pretend to be more competent and talented than you are. All you have to do is recognize the talents and qualities you have acquired throughout time. This recognition will help you recognize how awesome you are and will boost your self-esteem for those moments when you need to take a risk and believe in yourself to learn, grow, and improve.

• List five accomplishments that make you proud.

It is easy to lose sight of your past accomplishments when surrounded by negativity. Recognizing prior accomplishments allows you to see that you can do more in the future. Make a full report of each accomplishment. If you go beyond five, keep going until you run out of ideas. Life is a never-ending journey, a never-ending growth. You will often face difficulties that you have never faced before. You have two options for dealing with these challenges:

1. You may either believe that you are incapable of overcoming this new difficulty and so take a step back, or you can take a stride forward.

2. You recognize that you have conquered numerous problems in the past and can do it again.

3. You can't be confident that you'll succeed, but you also can't be positive that you won't. So, my thesis is that it is preferable to trust oneself and accept the challenge. Give it all you've got. Here is where self-esteem comes into play.

To have the requisite self-esteem, you must recognize that you have conquered significant problems in the past. You may boost your self-esteem by documenting and reflecting on your prior accomplishments. Most of the time, self-belief comes from understanding that you have accomplished remarkable things in the past. You have accomplished incredible things in your life; you just need to take the time to acknowledge them (Hofmann, 2007).

The Crucial Point: Again, this isn't about pretending to be someone you're not, as that would never work. Most individuals downplay their accomplishments while exaggerating their misfortunes. You only need to redress the balance by properly recognizing your many accomplishments.

• Describe three times when you overcame hardship.

Realising that you have the strength to deal with whatever life throws at you is one of the most important components of self-esteem. You may see that you can deal with challenging circumstances because of your previous successes in conquering hardship. Write a thorough narrative of the hardship you experienced and the abilities and traits you utilized to overcome it for each instance.

Remember that you are not required to stop at three.

In life, resilience is crucial. You must believe in your ability to accept and recover from adversity. The most resilient individuals will shrug it off when life throws adversity. They just recognize what needs to be done to get back on track and take the appropriate steps. All who lack resilience feel overwhelmed during difficult circumstances, and stress develops quickly because issues often linger for a long time.

Everyone can be resilient. Some individuals may not believe it since they cannot recollect earlier hardships they have conquered. Recognizing the challenges you've faced can build your resilience and enhance your self-esteem.

The Crucial Point: The confidence that you can overcome hardship is often the most critical aspect. This conviction stems from knowing that you have conquered adversity in the past. Everyone has conquered adversity in their lives; all you have to do is recall those instances.

• Name five people who have aided you.

Do not just name the five individuals; instead, offer a thorough narrative of how they assisted you. This thoroughness lets you realize that other people appreciate you and perceive your worth, and that is why they are eager to help you.

Continue counting if you have more than five.

The sense that others do not value you weighs heavily on your self-esteem. It is easy to lose trust when you believe you are alone and must handle life's issues independently. But the ancient adage "no man is an island" has a lot of truth. You will only ever be alone in this world ⁚ want to be. Even yet, it is difficult to avoid any human interaction will always be those willing to assist you when you need it. All you have to do is reach out to the right folks.

Recording all of the assistance you have gotten from others can boost your self-esteem since it will help you realise that you are not facing any challenges alone. You will know that you may ask for assistance and that, along with others who assist, you will be in a far better position to face any problem.

The Crucial Point: Receiving assistance from others when you are in need will always boost your self-esteem as it will convince you that you are a valuable person. Even if it occurred in the past, remembering occasions when people assisted you can boost your self-esteem.

• Name five people you've helped.

When you have poor self-esteem, you may believe that you are unimportant to others. This practice will help you realise that you have much more to contribute than before. Highlight how you assisted each individual and how they benefited from your assistance.

Don't stop at five if you have more of them.

It's easy to believe you have nothing valuable to give the world, yet this couldn't be farther from reality. Every day, you assist others. Sometimes the assistance you provide is substantial, but it can be tiny, yet it makes the other person's life a bit better and easier.

Consider the small ways people assist you and how much you value that assistance when you get it. That is how people react when you help them. The fact that you can assist others proves that you have something valuable to contribute. Take a minute to notice each time you assist someone else, and it will help boost your self-esteem.

The Crucial Point: Don't believe that to be valuable to others, you must make one enormous contribution to the world. People who make significant contributions to the world are admirable, but the small contributions and gestures given daily make the world run. So, recognize your worth and allow it to boost your self-esteem.

• Make a list of 50 positive aspects of your life.

Many individuals get gratitude and appreciation mixed up. Gratitude is just expressing gratitude to the other person for their assistance. Taking the time to appreciate means understanding how you benefited from your assistance. When you take the time to appreciate, you realize how lucky you are and see your life more positively.

As an example of gratitude, after a pleasant lunch at a restaurant, you may remark to your waiter that you appreciated their service. It may seem easy, but taking a moment to appreciate the advantage you got registers better with your brain than a quick thank you.

One of the most important things to grasp about expressing your gratitude is that it benefits both parties. By expressing your gratitude, you help the other person feel appreciated and realise how fortunate you are to have had a good experience.

The Crucial Point: You may not always have to show your gratitude to others, but continuously taking the time to appreciate the advantages you get can significantly boost your self-esteem. It would benefit both of you if you had the opportunity to show your thanks to others (Hallowell, 2022).

Although 50 may seem to be a large number, the goal here is to get you into the habit of enjoying it. And you may be shocked, but once you start discovering things to be grateful for, you'll want to keep going.

CHAPTER 8
SOCIAL SKILLS
IMPROVE CONVERSATIONS, FRIENDSHIPS, AND FULFILL RELATIONSHIPS WITHOUT GIVING UP WHO YOU ARE

Pe, with ADHD often report difficulties in social relationships, whether friendships, romantic relationships, business relationships, or familial relationships. It may be challenging to negotiate social interactions with those they know well, close friends, and strangers.

Most young adults build and develop social ties in their local surroundings, such as at school or college. Nevertheless, young individuals with ADHD prefer to form connections in their immediate surroundings, such as via parental associates or hanging out with friends. This may represent a desire for people to tap into more major social networks and, on occasion, establish friends with peers who are removed from school or are unemployed.

Individuals with ADHD must understand that showing themselves to others influences how others engage with them. This includes how individuals communicate with people and express themselves (verbal communication), their nonverbal posture and motions (body language), and the overall image they project (emotional expressions, ADHD features). This also entails developing social awareness and investigating the impact that any or all of these behaviors have on affecting other people's perspectives.

For instance, inattention to another person may misunderstand ADHD as a lack of interest in what the individual is saying. Adults with ADHD may also be viewed as erratic because they jump from one person to the next or from one subject of discussion to the next. Individuals with ADHD may be prone to making rash judgments and leaping to conclusions due to their impulsivity.

As a result, individuals may accept things at face value based on initial impressions and stereotypical influences. For example, if an acquaintance goes down a hallway without acknowledging them, they may quickly conclude that person does not like them and act in a manner that reflects this, resulting in a self-fulfilled prophecy (Hofmann, 2007). They may fail to consider other possibilities for the lack of recognition, such as the person being in a hurry and concerned with an important subject.

When working to develop your social skills, you must engage in the process correctly. Many individuals fail to enhance their social skills not because they face enormous hurdles but because they approach the work incorrectly and get frustrated. You'll make greater progress if you have the correct mindset, expectations, and attitude to improve.

This chapter discusses certain topics you should know before working on your problems. This chapter addresses some typical issues and concerns regarding developing one's social abilities.

DETERMINE WHICH TRAITS AND SKILLS TO WORK ON AND WHICH TO LEAVE ALONE

You don't have to alter everything about yourself to improve your social life. Of course, you'll want to address obvious issues that most people would like to avoid, such as shyness and nervousness, poor self-confidence, sloppy communication skills, and a lack of understanding of making friends. Nobody is socially perfect. They can still get by as long as they offer enough positives. If you come across any advice in this book that you disagree with, ask yourself, "Would skipping this tip make me happier overall?" Could I handle the penalties of failing to comply?"

For instance, maybe you're okay with having a franker communication style and also can deal with the reality that it will sometimes irritate certain individuals. Maybe you'll conclude you don't mind being moderately shy, even if it is officially an "issue."

DETERMINE WHAT WORKS BEST FOR YOU

When you consider the pros and drawbacks of a situation, you may decide that you should follow particular social traditions. For example, you'd never give fashion a second thought in your ideal world, but you understand other people do, so you learn to dress a bit better. Or you like spending a lot of time alone, but you force yourself to be around others a little more than you'd like to practice your interpersonal skills and spend time with your friends.

You must determine where you stand and whether or not you are ready to compromise. Changing is not an option if something contradicts your core principles or you just despise it. The practical method might work if you are apathetic about something, and it does not need much effort to accept it. However, there will always be aspects of the social environment in which you will be unable to participate, even if you recognize that it would be sensible. Most individuals will not abandon their religious or political beliefs to fit in.

For example, some men don't like sports but realise they'd have an easier time connecting with others if they did. Some people never grow to enjoy sports, but they can keep up with enough game outcomes and transactions to keep their discussions going. Others can't bring themselves to do even that, and they're content with the tiny inconveniences.

KEEP YOUR MIND OPEN

Although you don't have to entirely alter or sell yourself out to improve your social life, you should strive to retain an open mind. Be open to new experiences and the chance that you may acquire characteristics or grow to like things you never believed you would love one day.

People change during their life. It's crucial to be loyal to yourself, but not so much that you get stuck in your ways and reject everything new with "No, that's not who I am." Assume you've never danced before, and a buddy invites you to a beginner tango lesson.

Even if you suspect you won't get much out of it, it's too rigid to declare, "No, that's not me!" I don't enjoy dancing and will never like it!" You don't have to try everything that everyone advises, but you never know—you could like partner dancing and not realise it yet.

YOU CAN HAVE A SATISFYING SOCIAL LIFE WITHOUT FLAWLESS SOCIAL SKILLS

Many people have enjoyable social lives despite being a little timid and anxious, stumbling in their interactions, not having a lot of exciting interests, or having a few annoying personality flaws. Even the most charming individuals crack poor jokes or have their invitations declined. You don't have to master every ability in this book 100% of the time, and you don't have to win the approval of everyone on the earth.

You only need to be competent enough to get by and have people who accept you for who you are. You don't need every encounter to go perfectly. You simply need enough of them to go well to fulfill your social objectives (for example, if you ask ten people to hang out and only three respond, but they go on to become excellent friends, that's a success).

IMPROVING YOUR SOCIAL ABILITIES WITH PRACTICE

Social skills are much like any other talent. Reading tips may help you figure out what you need to focus on and make the learning process easier, but you still need to practice to get it down fully. You've spent fewer hours socializing than many of your friends, and you'll need to make up for the lost time.

That may seem apparent, yet some individuals believe social skills are acquired all at once by using the appropriate trick, insight, psychological "hack," or confidence booster when it comes to interpersonal skills. They probably believe this since social skills are non-physical and routine. People intuitively recognize that learning complicated physical talents such as skiing or sketching takes time. Their mind process is, "It's just chatting when it comes to socializing. That is something I am already familiar with. So just give me some secret super-effective conversation formulae, and I'll be all set."

Furthermore, most individuals have discovered that it is simpler to navigate a social setting when they are momentarily more confident than normal. So, there must be a method to be overconfident all of the time. However, although it is possible to feel extraordinarily confident for a short period of time, there is no way to summon that sensation or keep it for the rest of your life. There aren't any shortcuts. They'd be well known if there were, and this book wouldn't be necessary.

UNDERSTANDING WHAT YOU ARE WORKING ON AS YOU EXERCISE YOUR SOCIAL SKILLS

As you practice socializing, you will improve your general talents. You'll use just a few of them in certain situations, while others will demand you to juggle numerous at once.

I. Your quick-thinking capacity. When it's your moment to speak, you can't take long to formulate your answer. Aside from the somewhat predictable initial minute or two. It's impossible to think out what you're going t or how you'll handle every event ahead of time. The best you can do is study some broad rules and hone your improvisational skills.

2. Your multitasking abilities. When communicating with someone, you must constantly pay attention to many things at once. The other person continuously gives signals via their words, actions, and nonverbal communication. You must take it all in, assess, and determine how to respond to your findings on the fly ("They just mentioned they're not acquainted with cycling. I'll have to change the way I deliver my tale."). Simultaneously, you must regulate the signals ("I'm wondering what time it is, but I won't check my watch now since it may make me seem uninterested in their narrative."). As you get more adept at socializing, taking in all of that information and selecting what to do with it becomes less daunting.

3. Your ability to do a range of specific sub-skills such as listening, exerting yourself, or framing an invitation. When you listen carefully, express yourself, or give an invitation, you'll be sloppy and dramatic at first. Still, with practice, you'll acquire a deeper touch and be able to adapt your conduct to the scenario at hand. For example, when you're initially learning how to listen, you can come off as an over-the-top therapist. With further experience, you'll be able to demonstrate your concern and attentiveness more subtly.

4. Your degree of comfort with several subskills, such as creating eye contact and initiating discussions. Like establishing eye contact or starting a conversation, some subskills can seem awkward or strange at first, but the more you practice them, the more natural they will feel.

5. Your overall understanding of people, what makes them move, and how they respond to certain situations. Everyone is unique, but with enough social experience, you'll begin to recognize broad trends that you may act on. For example, you may observe that individuals who like a certain pastime have similar political opinions and communication styles, and you may modify them appropriately.

6. Your understanding of different social situations and how to manage them. This understanding may be learned by direct experience or by watching those more socially skilled than you. It is easy to get guidance on typical situations, such as how to greet people at a party or decline an outrageous request. Still, you will encounter other scenarios that are too uncommon and obscure to end up in any book in your daily life. When you encounter these unexpected circumstances, you may not always manage them precisely, but you may develop an overall understanding of how to approach them over time.

7. Your understanding of the unwritten social standards of your specific culture, subculture, or group of friends and how to modify basic commu-nication-skills principles to meet them. These unwritten social standards are another reason it is hard to anticipate how to handle every scenario. What is a pleasant conversation style in one culture or among one group of friends may be deemed irritating in another. The only way to under-stand the laws of your social environment is to immerse yourself in them and notice them for yourself.

8. Positive attitudes about socializing. A well-meaning but useless kind of social advice proposes adopting beneficial but easier-said-than-done mindsets such as, "Don't care too much about people's perceptions of you" or "Just go out to have fun and don't worry about how well you socialize." It's terrific if you can think like this, but you don't get such worldviews simply by reading about them. Instead, as you mingle more, you'll have numerous tiny achievements and experiences that demon-strate that these are healthy ways to think, and you'll gradually incorpo-rate them into your worldview.

9. Your own social style. There are broad principles for what constitutes a good or bad encounter, but no one correct method to socialize. Everyone has their personality and their own set of talents and shortcomings. There are generally many approaches to each scenario. What works wonderfully for someone else may not work for you at all. Your buddy may be skilled at cheering folks up by listening well. You could be better at making them laugh and distracting them from their troubles.

METHODS FOR PRACTISING SOCIALIZATION

There are three methods to practice your social skills. If you believe you are socially inexperienced, you may just discover methods to spend more time socializing. This technique is unstructured, but you will still learn new things and refine a range of talents due to the additional hours you will put in. You can:

• Increase your socialization with individuals you already know (existing friends, colleagues, classmates, housemates, and family members).

• Find a job that requires a lot of connection with people (such as retail, restaurant waiter, bartender, call center, or sales).

• Sign up for a socializing volunteer role (fundraising, chatting to the elderly, or assisting at a festival).

• Participate in a club, team, or organization.

• Attend online-organized meetings

• Utilize realistic chances for quick, polite conversations with individuals expected to be cheerful and converse with you, such as shop clerks and restaurant waiters.

• Go to a place where individuals may come alone and socialize with other customers (for example, a board game café, a bar, or a pool hall).

• Engage with others online (for example, chatting with people while playing a multiplayer game). Of course, this cannot be a total replacement for face-to-face practice, but it should not be rejected altogether; instead, if travel is a viable possibility, stay in busy, sociable hostels.

A second strategy is to practice a purposeful, organized manner, particularly useful when working on certain talents. If you have problems beginning conversations, you might attend one online-organized meet-up each week and chat with at least five new individuals each time.

If you're having problems with a certain form of encounter, such as asking someone out or saying no to an excessive request, you may practice with a friend or family member. Some organizations, including counseling agencies, provide social skills training groups that allow participants to practice in a safe and supportive atmosphere.

The third option for social practice is to enroll in a class to master performance-oriented interpersonal skills such as public speaking, acting, improv, or stand-up comedy. However, these highly specialized talents may not often translate well into everyday circumstances. A practiced, memorized speech is not the same as a casual, unscripted discussion. Nonetheless, they provide several advantages. Speech training, for example, may teach you how to project your voice and employ confident body language. Taking part in a play may help you overcome your anxiety and dread of being put on the spot. Improv encourages you to be more relaxed, fun, and spontaneous in your interactions. Many individuals feel that knowing they're getting the hang of a scarier ability, such as public speaking, gives them a tiny confidence boost in their regular contacts.

You don't need to spend a lot of time in public chatting to strangers to improve your social skills. Some individuals believe they must engage in casual conversation with strangers at the mall or grocery store. It's one thing to attempt to become accustomed to the beginning and carry on conversations with individuals you don't know.

Talking to strangers is frequently too unpleasant and ineffective if you want to gain social experience in general. Practicing with individuals you already know and are relatively comfortable with rather than strangers you meet in more organized environments such as an art class is preferable.

GETTING A BASIC FEEL FOR CONVERSATIONS

Conversations need effort. Even those who are naturally extroverted and seem to be able to speak to anybody become tongue-tied from time to time. So you're not alone if you don't feel comfortable striking up a discussion. Conversations are when the skill aspect of "social skills" truly comes into play since they need you to think on the fly. Three things influence how successfully your encounters go:

• How comfortable and confident you are in them.

• Your technical conversational abilities.

• Your general personality, interests, values, and points of view.

When individuals struggle to strike up a conversation, one of their most common complaints is that they "don't know what to speak about" or "always run out of things to say." This section provides general tips for keeping your interactions continuing.

DETERMINE YOUR CONVERSATIONAL OBJECTIVES

If you put the typical person in the cockpit of a fighter aircraft and instructed them to go through the start-up procedure and take off as soon as possible, they'd sit there dumbfounded because they wouldn't know where to begin. For the same reason, some individuals become blank during chats.

They find themselves conversing with someone and are aware that they must "make nice conversation," but they are unsure what to do next. It's simpler to speak to people if you have a general notion of where you want to take the conversation. If you feel yourself going blank, you may immediately remind yourself of one of the objectives, which should help you come up with something to say:

DAY-TO-DAY SOCIALIZING OBJECTIVES

Goal #1: Have a positive engagement for everyone involved.

Goal #2: Learn about the other person and attempt to discover common ground.

Goal #3: Tell the other person something about yourself.

Goal #4: Show you're a friendly person with social skills

Examples

• If you already know the individual, catch up on what you've been up to since your previous meeting (for example, happenings in your life, fun or engaging activities you've done, current issues on your mind).

• If you run into a colleague in the break room, have a quick, polite chat to demonstrate that you're a friendly person who works well with others.

• Before the book club meeting, discuss a subject dictated by the environment, such as what else you've been reading.

MAKE A GENERAL APPROACH TO CREATING CONVERSATION

Good conversationalists often use the tactics listed below. You may use the same tactics more purposefully. A comprehensive game plan may assist since it simplifies and explains what you need to think about, gives confidence that you're utilizing a system that works, and provides some solid, uncomplicated beginning material for practice.

It's a good idea to have many techniques ready to go so that if one fails, you may try another. You may also flip between broad methods as a discussion progresses. You do not have to use the same method for every individual or scenario.

One technique to offer yourself some direction is to inquire about their interests ("I'm going to ask about their hobbies and attempt to identify one we share in common," for example). ("My grandfather is curious about what I've been up to recently, so I'll concentrate on telling him what's new in my life since I last saw him"). Here are some other ways to consider:

Approach #1: Be interested in and curious about other people and make it your aim to discover what makes them intriguing and distinctive.

Approach #2: Discuss the other person's interests.

Approach #3: Determine what subjects you like discussing and then attempt to lead the discussion.

THE PROCESS OF MAKING FRIENDS

You've arrived at the chapter's last part, which outlines how to meet friends, develop a social life, and overcome loneliness. Even if you're the kind of person who enjoys spending time alone, you'll feel lonely if your lesser need for social interaction isn't fulfilled. Loneliness may erode your happiness and feeling of self-worth. It's disheartening to spend the seventh Friday night in a row by yourself.

The good news is that learning how to create friends is pretty simple; if you lack an understanding of how to build friendships, you may see some effects right away if you learn and implement the techniques. If you can control your shyness and have a conversation, you should be able to apply the suggestions in this area to enhance your social life.

The fundamentals of building friends:

1. Find potential friends.

2. Invite and plan to do something with those potential friends.

3. Once you've established some new friends, take the relationships to the next level.

4. Repeat the preceding stages until you've created as many friends as possible, whether it's a small group of close friends or a large number.

People who struggle with their social life miss one or more of these stages.

STEP 1 - FINDING POTENTIAL FRIENDS

The first stage in creating friends is to seek potential friends. That's a prominent place to start, yet it's where some lonely individuals get stuck.

They don't expose themselves to enough new prospective pals. This chapter discusses the two primary methods for finding prospects: using your existing connections and meeting new individuals.

MAKE USE OF YOUR CURRENT CONTACTS

If you've recently moved to a new region and don't know anybody, drawing on your present connections won't work, but you'll frequently find the seeds of social life. You are not required to go out and meet hundreds of people. It is often simpler to convert current connections into full-fledged friends than to find new ones. You could already know a few individuals who might become part of your new social circle.

• Individuals from work or school with whom you get along but have never hung out; acquaintances with whom you're amicable when you run into each other but never see otherwise.

• Friends of individuals you know who you've bonded with when you've met in the past; persons who have shown an interest in becoming your buddy in the past but you never accepted the offer; folks you only meet on occasion but could see more regularly.

• Friends with whom you've lost contact; cousins who live nearby and are your age.

MEET NEW PEOPLE

Getting more out of your present relationships might be beneficial, but it isn't always possible. Fortunately, there are many locations where you may meet new individuals. Before we get started, here are some things to bear in mind while looking for new friends.

For instance, you'll probably have to pull yourself out of your routine and prioritize meeting new people. Some lonely individuals slip into a rut where they are comfortable at home when not at work or school.

You may have to try a few different places to meet people before finding one that works for you. Finding new acquaintances is often one of those circumstances when putting in 20% of the work yields 80% of the rewards. You may attend multiple meetups, workshops, or events and find that they are all a flop, but you might easily meet many great people at the next one.

STEP 2 – MAKE A PLAN FOR SOMETHING TO DO

One early planning stumbling point for some individuals is knowing who they want to hang out with but not knowing where to invite them. It's also very unusual for socially inexperienced individuals to claim that they have no idea what others their age do when they get together. Hanging out with other people is usually about spending time with them.

Don't assume that spending time with somebody is all about planning the perfect event for them to attend. Don't assume there's no purpose in hanging out with them if you can't come up with anything great to do. When you choose to hang out with someone, you are mostly there to enjoy their company. Of course, seeing a band or going on a walk makes your time together more pleasant and memorable, but it's not necessarily required.

Inviting folks to a gathering is frequently more about conducting variants on a few tried-and-true activities than coming up with something unique each time. If you like your friend's company, you may easily spend several weeks hanging out at their place or going to the same rotation of cafés or bars, with just the odd, more exciting event tossed in to change things up.

CREATE AN INVITATION

After you've decided on an activity, you must ask everyone whether they want to participate.

If someone decides to accept your invitation, it will be because they want to spend time with you and the planned activity interests them, and is accessible. It makes no difference whether you inquired in person, text message, or phone call. Choose the approach that is most convenient for you. On the other hand, group invites are simpler to plan by sending out a single email to which everyone may respond.

Invite folks out in a non-pressuring tone: "It'd be wonderful if you came, but if you don't, that's okay."

METHODS FOR MAKING NEW FRIENDSHIPS

Every friendship is unique, and not every element will relate to every kind in the same way. Some friendships are built on sharing and connecting, while others are built on hobbies, humor, and going out.

• Spend more time with each other.

• Spend one-on-one time with them.

• Maintain contact with them in between hangouts.

• Have a wonderful time while you hang out together.

• Learn more about each other and broaden your conversation subjects. Be a nice friend in all the typical ways.

• Be there for them in their moments of need.

• Have some fun and go on some adventures together.

HAVE FULFILLING RELATIONSHIPS WITHOUT GIVING UP WHO YOU ARE

To have a meaningful relationship, you must devote time and energy to developing the connection and your personal development and self-growth. One cannot exist without the other. The secret formula to having a fulfilling and exciting relationship is to engage in the connection and your own growth. A fulfilling relationship has two parties who invest in their personal growth as much as they do in the partnership's progress.

Small, incremental changes will dramatically revolutionize your relationship. You must take many actions before seeing huge improvements in your relationship. These actions are both beneficial and exciting for the partnership. This enthusiasm motivates you both to make a good life. Not only will your relationship benefit from the minor improvements, but so will you in your personal life.

LIVE FREE OF EXPECTATIONS

Don't demand your partner to do anything merely to make you happy.

Wanting your partner to do a certain activity for you to be happy is a toxic way of thinking. How would you feel if your spouse expected you to call as soon as you got home from work? You would probably feel some pressure, and nobody likes feeling forced to do anything. If you didn't feel obligated, you'd be happy to contact your partner after work. Put yourself in your partner's shoes. If you expect your spouse to make you happy constantly, your life will never be truly fulfilled.

A relationship is a link formed by two people who have something to offer each other. You can't expect your spouse to be your only source of happiness. You must take responsibility for your happiness and allow your spouse to contribute. A satisfying relationship occurs when both persons contribute to the enjoyment of the other without any expectations. You are the one who determines whether you are happy or sad. Don't put that choice in the hands of your spouse. Remember that your relationship can only help you be happy.

CONCENTRATE ON CORRECTING YOUR FLAWS

Instead of pointing out your partner's weaknesses, examine yourself first.

It's our nature to point out the defects of others before examining our own. To have a good relationship, you must recognize the value of concentrating on overcoming your defects rather than pointing out your partner's problems. We all have flaws; it's part of who we are. When you and your partner argue, look inside yourself before focusing on your partner's weaknesses. You will become judgemental and critical if you concentrate too much on your partner's weaknesses. This focus on your partner's weaknesses just erodes the basis of your connection.

Instead of pointing the finger at your spouse the next time you dispute, point the finger at yourself and ask, "What do I need to work on?" It might be the capacity to completely listen to your partner's point of view or the ability to be less obstinate and hardheaded. Whatever the case may be, turn to yourself for the answer rather than your companion. If you continue to concentrate on your partner's weaknesses, you will just be treading water. Make the decision now to begin concentrating on your growth, and this will help not just you but also your relationship.

KEEP THINGS COOL

When your spouse does anything that irritates you, don't respond instantly.

Attacking your spouse right away after they have upset you will only make matters worse. Consider the phrase "the quiet before the storm." This is the era of serenity and tranquillity before a period of conflict and sorrow. I know from personal experience how simple it is to lash out at your spouse when they irritate you. Patience and the capacity to deliberately stop oneself from negatively responding are required. It will not be a quick remedy; rather, it will be a long-term behavioral shift. Your actions will either exacerbate or diminish the storm's effect. It's all up to you.

Remember that if you continue to respond to your spouse whenever they upset you negatively, they are more inclined to conceal anything that would upset you. Do you want to build a foundation founded on secrets and lies? I'm certain you don't. Try to take deep breaths and actively prevent yourself from negatively responding. Understand your partner's perspective and communicate in a manner that is successful and promotes constructive discourse. Commit to building a firm foundation of trust, dedication, and patience.

BE INTERESTED IN YOUR PARTNER

Whatever problems you face, make it a habit to be interested in your relationship and their needs. I've established this in my own marriage. My spouse and I sit on the sofa every evening after work and ask each other thought-provoking questions. These questions help us both understand each other better. Never let life's stresses take over your relationship. Continue to push back on stress and build the basis of your connection.

Have you ever wondered why young toddlers are so interested in life? They are eager to share what they have learned about the world. A young child's interest and enthusiasm should drive you to do the same with your spouse. Be interested in learning more about your companion. What piques their interest? What brings them joy? What causes them to cry? Questions like these will assist you in creating a vibrant love map of your companion.

BE EAGER FOR PERSONAL GROWTH

Maintain a constant flow of ideas about how to grow and develop as an individual and as a pair.

We are all lifetime students. You can learn something new even if you're 87 years old. Every day should be a chance for you to grow, develop, and enhance your life knowledge, and this involves both your development and the growth of your partnership. Read personal development and relationship books to get insights into living a better life.

Did you know that the average commuter in the United States spends 38 hours a year stuck in traffic? Instead of worrying about traffic, listen to an audio program on personal growth or marriage. Listening to an audio program reduces your stress level and increases your knowledge.

The energy of a relationship affects both people. Every day, feed this energy with inspiration. Look for methods to improve yourself and your relationship regularly. Never, ever stop learning because if you stop, you stop developing.

CHAPTER 9
HEALTH AND WELLBEING

ADHD is defined as difficulty planning and maintaining effort throughout time to attain a good objective in the future under the executive function/motivational deficit hypothesis of ADHD and anxiety. This chapter focuses on the long-term effect of adult ADHD and anxiety on the central aspects of health and well-being management across time.

Although improving health habits cannot be considered therapies for ADHD, unhealthy behaviors may impact ADHD and amplify symptoms of the illness. Therefore, creating healthy habits offers a solid treatment objective and a necessity for an overall wellness approach for treating anxiety and ADHD.

SLEEP

People with ADHD who experience anxiety often report difficulties with their sleep's beginning, quantity, and quality. Although most individuals can get through the day after a bad night's sleep, the situation is sometimes more difficult for those with ADHD and anxiety.

The effects on well-being grow more obvious when sleep issues become more regular and persistent. Inadequate sleep is connected with less attention, more distractibility, and more significant problems staying focused in work, lectures, discussions, and awake. It affects numerous other self-regulatory features - the opposite of what people with ADHD and anxiety need.

Furthermore, a disruption of the sleep cycle has a detrimental influence on other biological systems, such as hunger and mood, and is linked to increased cancer risk. The advantages of being a "night person" should be added to the many misconceptions about ADHD, besides "hyperfocus" and "multitasking."

Chronic sleep issues resemble ADHD and anxiety in appearance. In reality, some people with untreated fundamental sleep problems, such as sleep apnea, may wrongly believe they have ADHD or anxiety. In contrast, many people with a history of ADHD and anxiety also have sleep difficulty, with one of these clinical conditions exacerbating the other.

Most people with ADHD and anxiety identify poor sleep as a direct result of ADHD symptoms. The most prevalent challenges are "trouble turning down my thoughts" or "procrastinating on sleep," mainly staying up late to watch television, play computer games, or participate in other online activities despite physical exhaustion. When these conditions continue for a long enough period, the sleep-wake cycle will shift.

Exposure to sunshine helps one remain awake and attentive throughout the day, while the lack of light at night relates to the brain's melatonin production, which aids in sleep. People perform better when they maintain a morning circadian orientation, in which they arise in the morning, are active throughout the day, and sleep at night.

Individuals with ADHD and anxiety have a progressive change to an abnormal evening circadian orientation. This self-identification as a night owl is adopted to rationalize and perpetuate the maladaptive sleep-wake cycle, which affects the body's regulating mechanisms.

As you would expect, getting enough sleep is a critical step in controlling ADHD, and most individuals underestimate the extent to which inadequate sleep impairs performance. Returning to a theme of this guidebook, you likely tell yourself that going to bed at a decent hour is vital. Still, each night, you find yourself remaining online or doing anything else far later than anticipated. Perhaps you've given up on even attempting to go to bed at a reasonable hour. You aim to get more sleep every day, but you don't have a viable strategy.

The first step is to prioritize sleep like a job. That is, rather than describing sleep as being up and busy until you can't keep your eyes open any longer, it becomes a specific activity that you "do" ("I will go to bed at 10 pm").

To determine your bedtime, first determine when you must get up in the morning and then count back by the number of hours you need for a full night's sleep (not the least amount to "get by"), establishing specified sleep and waking periods.

Your daily planner is a tool that helps you to objectively examine your obligations and estimate the time you need to get out of bed every morning to get ready for school, work, or other responsibilities. Even if you do not have an early morning start, such as a scholar whose first class is not until noon or a worker on the second shift, you surely notice that you spend a lot of time in bed yet do not feel rested. We recommend that you set a goal time for beginning your day and arrange your day around that time.

Work backward by eight or nine hours from your actual wake-up time to determine when you should go to bed. There are several exceptions, such as someone who understands that seven hours of sleep is plenty or a working single mother of three children whose obligations do not allow her that much sleep time. You will need to change this number to reflect the reality of your life, but we also urge that you analyze and dispute the notion that "there is no way I can get into bed and fall asleep any sooner." We recommend that you focus on adaptive sleep ideas.

You are an autonomous, free-thinking adult who will make your own choices about how to live your life. However, we urge you to experiment for at least one week – preferably two – to evaluate whether feeling more rested helps you operate better throughout the day. You may discover that what you can achieve during the day—both work/academic and recreational—satisfies you more than what you do late at night rather than sleeping. This experiment requires you to adjust your evening habits and test your belief that you are an unchanging night person.

Consider how you sleep. In truth, sleeping is more of a set of actions you engage in that put your body and brain in a state that permits you to fall asleep. Following the establishment of your goal sleep periods, the next phase in "doing" sleep is breaking the task down into a series of sleep-promoting behavioral tasks that you carry out. These techniques will teach and cue your body and brain to sleep more swiftly and effortlessly over time and with repetition.

A nocturnal regimen is required, just as it is for children. You must also choose a "get into bed" time whenever you choose to begin your sleep cycle. Some individuals know that they fall asleep easily as soon as their head strikes the pillow, and they may not need a ritual other than committing to going to bed. Others need a long time lying in bed before falling asleep because they have difficulty relaxing or quieting their brains.

It is beneficial to have a consistent routine before going to bed to help you wind down your day and prepare for sleep. Start by getting ready for the following day at work or school, packing book bags and meals for the kids, or turning off lights and placing things away. Preparing your coffee maker or putting out the clothing you'll wear to work the following day are fantastic time saves that also help fuel your "sleep script."

We recommend setting aside or disconnecting from computers, smartphones, and devices at least 90 minutes before bed. These devices will prompt justifications for breaking your sleep schedule ("I only need to check a few emails before bed," or "I'll watch one more episode of this show.").

There is substantial evidence that the blue light produced by computers, tablets, and smartphone displays fools your brain into thinking it is daytime, interfering with your brain's generation of sleep-promoting melatonin.

In addition to suppressing melatonin, the bright illumination makes it harder to wind down the body's activity and alter body temperature as a component of the sleep onset phase. Delayed Sleep Phase Syndrome affects more than half of individuals with ADHD. On electronic devices, you can employ several applications and other illumination modifications to help wind yourself down if you choose to continue using electronics near bedtime.

Spending time doing something calming will help you fall asleep faster. Many individuals feel that reading fulfills this purpose, while others complain that they get too engrossed in a book. We recommend gathering some go-to sleep reading materials, such as a dull course book, a book with numerous short chapters, or a book you adore but have read so many times that you can simply leave it aside.

You can also use old magazines that you've read multiple times. Some of our patients conduct stretching exercises or light yoga before going to bed. You can also use relaxation techniques before going to bed or lying down.

It is worthwhile to mention a few words about relaxing and managing ADHD and anxiety. We address thoughtful acceptance and the capacity to withstand some pain when confronted with activities, and this guidance also applies to enhancing sleep. You may not feel sleepy after your bedtime routine, but it does not indicate your strategy is ineffective or that you are not exhausted. ADHD impairs your capacity to self-monitor, causing you to be distracted from paying attention to your body and its indications, such as weariness.

The sleep pattern provides a framework for training your brain and body to maintain a better sleep schedule. So, mindful acceptance acknowledges that your body is relaxing even if you are not yet sleeping. Furthermore, resting in bed is more relaxing than doing other things that keep you awake and engaged.

You may practice relaxing techniques while resting in bed. Distracting your mind from day-to-day troubles and controlling your breathing, such as inhaling and exhaling for particular counts, are the basic components of relaxation. That is all that is required.

Having a neutral picture in your mind, such as a color, and gently accepting a troubling notion helps calm your mind. Keeping your breathing pattern slow and regular helps to keep your body calm. To relieve muscular tension, concentrate on relaxing your muscles and allowing your bed to hold you.

These sleep tips – such as having an early cut-off time for caffeine consumption, exercising during the day (but not too close to bedtime), and not watching the clock if you wake up during the night – are all things you can do to enhance your sleep and reboot your circadian schedule. If you take a stimulant medication for ADHD or anxiety, you should talk to your doctor about the time of your final dosage and how it can influence your sleep.

You must:

1. Make sleep a top priority.

2. Establish the time you must be up in the morning.

3. Work backward from the number of hours of sleep you need to determine when you should go to bed. Write down this sleep time in your daily planner.

4. Create a sleep pattern that encourages you to enter "sleep mode." This pattern might involve arranging your clothing and other belongings for the following day, putting away devices 90 minutes before bed, reading or indulging in other soothing activities, etc.

5. Follow conventional sleep hygiene rules throughout the day, such as no coffee after a certain time, limiting alcohol usage, sleeping exclusively in

your bed, avoiding activity too late in the day, keeping the bedroom at a suitable temperature, and limiting daytime naps, etc.

6. Be aware of sleep-related cognitive mistakes. Even if you get a bad night's sleep, you will have enough energy the following day to perform effectively, even if you are not at your best.

7. If you wake up at night, avoid looking at the time.

8. If you have trouble falling back asleep, get out of bed for ten minutes and read or sit quietly before returning to bed.

EXERCISE

It will be no surprise that exercise has several health advantages, including enhanced sleep. Exercise has been linked to specific advantages for individuals with ADHD and anxiety, such as time-limited increases in concentration and mood. Exercise can reverse – and ideally avoid – certain concerning health patterns observed in research that follows children with ADHD as they enter adulthood.

Aside from continuing ADHD symptoms into adulthood, these people have risk factors for coronary heart disease due to their lifestyle choices. Although these trends are not conclusive, individuals with ADHD are more likely to have sedentary lifestyles, have poor eating habits, and participate in harmful activities such as nicotine use. Correspondingly, you should find a strategy to maintain a healthy level of exercise.

Let us distinguish between health and fitness. It is possible to be healthy without being physically fit. The purpose of exercise does not have to improve one's physical fitness or athletic ability, while these are good goals that inspire some individuals. Rather, we hope you outline a realistic health habit in particular words, concentrate on the initial steps to get started, and then make appointments with yourself to carry out this plan (with a start time and an end time). Presumably, you will be able to build and maintain this fitness routine over time.

Simple, quick, and inexpensive is a technique to find plans that you are more likely to start and maintain. Walking is a simple habit that most individuals can adopt. There are numerous ways to begin a walking plan without significantly altering your current routine. These include taking the stairs at work, walking to work, walking during breakfast or other breaks, or taking your dog for a long walk when you get home from work.

Committing to someone else, like walking your dog or organizing walks with a colleague or spouse, encourages follow-through and strengthens connections. Signing up for a yoga class or joining a softball team, for example, holds you responsible for others and enhances the probability that you will stick to your plan. You may prefer alternative types of exercise, such as biking or going to the gym three days a week. The goal is to discover an activity or a menu of activities that you can stick with.

"I don't have time" is a common justification for not beginning an exercise routine. Rather than assuming this, study your daily planner and ask yourself, "When do I have time to squeeze in some exercise?" Again, defining the sort of activity in mind is beneficial. Even if you can't afford the time or money to attend the gym, you can find ways to get some extra walking in throughout the day, even if it means taking the stairs instead of the elevator at work or parking at the far end of the parking lot at work or a shop.

Of course, exercising is one of those jobs that are especially prone to procrastination and a slew of negative ideas like "I'm too tired," "I'm not in the game to work out," and "I'll do it tomorrow." We often use exercise as an example to illustrate typical procrastination circumstances and cognitions (independent of ADHD status).

Identifying and challenging these procrastinating ideas is critical: "I'm exhausted after work, but I know that I'll feel better and more invigorated once I get started," she says. "No one is ever in the mood to work out." "Let me concentrate on turning off the TV, getting up, and changing into my workout clothes," and "I'm exaggerating the drawbacks of exercise while discounting the rewards." "I'll exercise for at least 15 minutes, and if that's all I can do today, I'll call it a day." Remembering and factoring in the great sensations you receive throughout the exercise and the joy of finishing it is beneficial.

People frequently ask us how long it takes for a habit to form. We cannot offer a clear answer, but we have discovered that two weeks—two work weeks and two weekends—is a reasonable baseline. We advise you to test a healthy activity, such as a daily walk, to see whether it may become more regular and need less effort to accomplish.

HEALTHY EATING

Maintaining healthy eating habits is a fantastic strategy to enhance general health and provide the groundwork for improved ADHD and anxiety management. Food choices, paying close attention to when and how much you eat, and coping with impulsivity are aspects of good eating pertinent to ADHD and anxiety. Individuals on stimulant drugs for ADHD or anxiety may experience appetite suppression, a frequent adverse effect of this type of medication.

Reduced appetite in children or teenagers using ADHD meds needs close monitoring to ensure they obtain adequate calories and nutrients. Young people, especially those in college, must be cautious of their diets and food consumption. Even if there is no health or nutrition problem, poor self-monitoring, planning, and impulsivity may lead to an overreliance on unhealthy convenience meals. Adults with ADHD and anxiety may also underestimate the impact of increased hunger and blood sugar drops on mood, impulsive control, and focus.

It is beneficial to ensure that you have something to eat at each of the three conventional meal times, even if it is a modest quantity. Similarly, keeping nutritious snacks nearby, such as crackers or granola bars, can supply you with enough nutrition and energy to keep you going until you can have a real meal or at least a more substantial snack.

Staying hydrated is another key issue since inadequate self-monitoring may put you at risk for dehydration, making you feel ill even in moderate cases. Because the dry mouth is a typical side effect of many drugs, water provides a simple, healthful, zero-calorie alternative.

When it comes to healthy eating, stimulus management is key. Making educated decisions about the foods you have on hand is a sort of environmental engineering. If you don't have any ice cream in your freezer, you don't have to decide whether to eat that late-night bowl of ice cream. These procedures need planning to locate healthy alternatives (like crunchy fruit instead of crunchy potato chips). Include these appropriate health behavior activities in your overall coping strategy.

We don't want you to have an all-or-nothing attitude toward eating or believe that individuals with ADHD and anxiety can't have certain guilty pleasures. However, you must be cautious not to exploit Ben Franklin's motto, "moderation in all things—including moderation," to justify reckless action. You can adjust your eating habits despite allegations that you are a "junk food addict," just as you can create sleep patterns after becoming a night person.

We recommend that you begin the change process by concentrating on a single implementation goal, enhancing one healthy habit and lowering one problematic behavior. For example, for one week, purchase apples (or a variety of fruits) as your healthy snack instead of potato chips (or other bad snack food). Another option is to make a healthy substitution within a snack meal, such as unbuttered microwave popcorn instead of the mega-ultra theatre-artery-clogging-style-butter type.

Similarly to overcoming procrastination to begin work, you will likely discover that you have increased your eating pleasure in a healthy alternative after choosing a healthy option. The goal is not to exclude everything but the most nutritious items from your diet but instead to make educated eating choices, modify your eating habits in a better direction, and reduce the negative impacts of impulsivity on your well-being.

HARMFUL HABITS AND HOW TO CHANGE THEM

ADHD and anxiety are linked to an increased risk of drug use disorders, notably alcohol, marijuana, or nicotine use. Caffeine may also be used excessively, with many young people utilizing highly caffeinated energy drinks to self-medicate symptoms and to remain up to combat the consequences of poor sleep patterns.

Several paths lead to the formation of these undesirable behaviors. Your family of origin may have exposed you to these behaviors, indicating a hereditary predisposition for drug abuse. Peer pressure may magnify impulsivity, leading to teenage drug use and continuing as self-medicine for the undiagnosed ADHD. Whatever the cause, these habits cause issues in your life and make managing ADHD much more difficult.

In a full-fledged drug or alcohol addiction, the first step is to seek treatment for the addiction via a detoxification program. It is believed that 25% of people in treatment programs have a background of ADHD. Even though ADHD is the apparent cause that puts you at risk for these issues, you need to be clean and sober before treating the ADHD symptoms with drugs, psychosocial therapy, or other methods. A history of addiction and the possibility of associated mood or anxiety disorders complicates your clinical position and treatment demands, including monitoring your risk of relapse.

Most readers' drug use, if it occurs at all, will not be of the frequency or volume that necessitates inpatient recovery or even comes close to being termed an addiction. However, you may notice certain troublesome behaviors that interfere with your ability to control ADHD and serve as distractions or escape routes. Thus, you may use marijuana or alcohol to cope with stress or racing thoughts when trying to sleep. Still, these behaviors may also keep you trapped in a cycle of procrastination, denial, and under-function. Likewise, excessive dependence on nicotine or caffeine may improve your capacity to concentrate on a task in the short term, but it may have health consequences that exceed the advantages.

Recognizing these harmful practices as contributing to your coping issues is the first step in dealing with your ADHD more directly. Once in therapy, these behaviors are often targeted for correction. Medications for ADHD that lower fundamental symptoms should help you better handle activities. You won't need to use drugs to escape the tension and other emotions.

You must:

1. Get enough sleep.

2. Prioritize a decent amount of activity/exercise in your daily schedule.

3. Concentrate on developing at least one good eating behavior and eliminating one harmful eating habit.

4. Plan and track your health activities using your daily planner.

5. Be proactive in obtaining care for changes in symptoms caused by menstrual cycles, pregnancy, early menopause, or menopause in women.

6. Engage in safe sex, including birth control devices that protect against sexually transmitted diseases.

7. Monitor and make efforts (including seeking therapy) to eliminate harmful habits, such as nicotine and excessive caffeine use.

FINAL THOUGHTS

We've discussed the definition, causes, and treatments for social anxiety. This book has provided simple yet solid and practical ways for dealing with social anxiety and ADHD, allowing you to make changes in your life that will bring you peace and pleasure. You've also learned a little bit about my own life and how I'm now using my experiences to assist others.

You now understand what social anxiety is and how powerful it can be in a person's life. You should also understand the notion that happy thoughts attract favorable outcomes, while negative mental pictures just serve to bring more negativity into your life. You've also discovered that you can construct your own life and that your ideas shape the life you live.

You must use all of the information and practices you have read in this book for it to be effective. You must utilize all of them, even if they are not in the sequence we have listed in this book.

You are now aware of the need to know and have decided to conquer social anxiety by writing down your goals for your life. The next step would be to request what you want. It is critical to believe in what you desire and have decided on, and you should not allow any doubts to seep in afterward.

Always think about what you want and think positively. Any negative thinking will erode the gains you've accomplished. Last but not least, you now understand the power of thankfulness. Always express gratitude for everything in your life. More importantly, keep in mind that you must strive and act toward your intended objectives for the transition to be effective. No miracles exist.

Begin immediately with small actions that will enable you to apply the tactics to your advantage properly. Undoubtedly, conquering social anxiety is proven to alter lives; it is up to you to choose an area of your life or what you desire and request the universe to begin the process of transformation. Make more inquiries and do other research to broaden your understanding of social anxiety and the strategies presented here.

You must have a clear mind to benefit from this book. You must cultivate habits that will assist you in achieving your aim for mental clarity, leaving you healthier, happier, and more successful. You will obtain success, pleasure, personal satisfaction, and excellent health by thinking clearly.

When you can't think clearly, you often make bad judgments. Anxiety develops due to being continually doubtful or concerned, and the resulting stress leads to ill health. Indeed, clear thinking is essential for personal happiness and wellness.

You must discover how to enhance your health for improved mental clarity by cultivating your existing abilities and making changes in your life that obscure your judgment. Clear thinking has been characterized as the capacity to think clearly and intelligently without being confused. It is being rational. Clear thinking, in my opinion, is having the presence of mind to successfully regulate your ideas, examine your thoughts, and ultimately make solid judgments.

To be a clear thinker, you must be able to process thoughts logically and in depth via independent and reflective thinking. It is more than just information acquisition since it does not only rely on memory. For increased knowledge and intelligent judgments, you must be capable of anticipating the implications of what you know.

Furthermore, clear thinking encompasses much more than just thinking; it comprises mental nurture, wellness, and the structuring of our life. Our ideas or thoughts ultimately decide who we become. Every day, you make various choices with far-reaching repercussions, all of which stem from the same source—your mind. Mental clarity and wellness are essential for making sound judgments. Clear thinking necessitates clear thinking. When your mind is congested, you are on edge and preoccupied, and you do very little.

A lot is going on in someone's head. As a result, you do not need to keep everything in your head. Get a tool to help you keep track of everything. This tool should function as a storage device for any information you do not want to forget. For instance, if you have an appointment or a future project, write it down or note it in your calendar. You might also maintain a more thorough diary. A notebook will allow you to get rid of everything that keeps you from getting things done, such as relationship issues, providing you peace of mind.

Let go of memories of errors made, individuals we have harmed, previous disappointments, and wasted chances. Most individuals cling to these memories and refuse to let them go. Memories that bring you down clog your mind and life, preventing you from thinking clearly.

When you decide to tackle a job, begin with the essential one and work your way down the list until the last one is completed. Take on no more than one job at a time, then set aside a certain amount of time to arrange everything. During that time, keep your thoughts clean and set aside everything that can distract you from work at hand.

Too much knowledge might clog your mind. This information that you take in daily from periodicals, newspapers, television, social media sites and the internet must be regulated. You may restrict the quantity of information you consume by determining how much time you devote to social media and other sources. Unsubscribe from online magazines and blogs that are of no use to you. Consider ideas from people you respect, and ultimately, disregard extraneous information.

Create a schedule for every part of your life and everything you do. This schedule will assist in lessening the amount of stress your brain has to deal with. Plan for the minor details ahead of time. Complete several tasks daily. You cannot, however, do everything. Make a list of the essential items and deal with them. It gives your mind time and space to think clearly.

Mental clutter obstructs our inner thoughts and stands in the way of clear thinking and focusing on what is essential. Begin by emptying your thoughts of useless items that take up mental space but bring no value or boost clear thinking.

Personal transformation must begin at the subconscious level; else, it will never occur. Improving our review is the key to changing our life and attaining what we want. Working on the subconscious to alter your thinking is as easy as imagining what you desire and concentrating on it for some time.

Working on the subconscious will almost certainly unlock the hidden power of your subconscious mind and help you acquire what you desire when you allow yourself. You're intended to attract things rather than chase them down, and the subconscious mind is the key to making that happen.

REFERENCES

Cuncic, A. (2021, February 19). Understanding the causes of social anxiety disorder. Verywell Mind. Retrieved May 18, 2022, from https://www.verywellmind.com/social-anxiety-disorder-causes-3024749

Hallowell, E. M., & Ratey, J. J. (2022). Adhd 2.0: New science and essential strategies for thriving with distraction--from childhood through adulthood. Ballantine Books.

Koyuncu, A., Ertekin, E., Yüksel, Ç., Aslantaş Ertekin, B., Çelebi, F., Binbay, Z., & Tükel, R. (2015). Predominantly inattentive type of ADHD is associated with social anxiety disorder. Journal of attention disorders, 19(10), 856-864.

Rodebaugh, T. L., Holaway, R. M., & Heimberg, R. G. (2004). The treatment of social anxiety disorder. Clinical Psychology Review, 24(7), 883-908.

Stein, M. B., & Stein, D. J. (2008). Social anxiety disorder. The Lancet, 371(9618), 1115-1125.

Weiss, G., & Hechtman, L. T. (1993). Hyperactive children grown up: ADHD in children, adolescents, and adults. Guilford Press.

Çelebi, F., & Ünal, D. (2021). Self esteem and clinical features in a clinical sample of children with ADHD and social anxiety disorder. Nordic Journal of Psychiatry, 75(4), 286-291.

CPSIA information can be obtained
at www.ICGtesting.com
Printed in the USA
BVHW080103031222
653304BV00011B/1233

9 781801 769754